T0299253

Corporate Governance Models

The activities carried out in a business organisation stem from the contribution of subjects who cooperate in the expectation of obtaining adequate rewards. The ability of organisations to reach a specific level of performance is influenced by the ownership structure, while the management is directed and controlled through a set of rules and incentives. This set regulates the distribution of rights and responsibilities among the board, company management and stakeholders and it defines the corporate governance model adopted by the organisation.

The collapse of global organisations across the world have undoubtedly revealed the inherent flaws in the contemporary corporate governance practices. As a result of these international scandals, a great deal of multidisciplinary research has been growing restlessly to define the specificities of each corporate governance model, however, lacking a specific investigation into the presumed existence of the most suitable one. By favouring the synthesis and the inductive procedure, this book analyses the potential existence of the most appropriate corporate governance model based on comparative international analysis of cultural, social and economic factors influencing the organisation's choice regarding the corporate governance model to be adopted.

This volume will be of interest to researchers, academics, professionals and students in the fields of corporate governance, international business and law.

Marco Mastrodascio is Post Doc Teaching Assistant at the University of Rome 'Tor Vergata' and Research Fellow at LUMSA University, Italy.

Routledge Focus on Business and Management

The fields of business and management have grown exponentially as areas of research and education. This growth presents challenges for readers trying to keep up with the latest important insights. *Routledge Focus on Business and Management* presents small books on big topics and how they intersect with the world of business research.

Individually, each title in the series provides coverage of a key academic topic, whilst collectively, the series forms a comprehensive collection across the business disciplines.

Conflict, Power, and Organizational Change
Deborah A. Colwill

Human Resource Management for Organisational Change
Theoretical Formulations
Dr. Paritosh Mishra, Dr. Balvinder Shukla and Dr. R. Sujatha

Human Resource Management and the Implementation of Change
Dr. Paritosh Mishra, Dr. Balvinder Shukla and Dr. R. Sujatha

Corporate Governance Models
A Critical Assessment
Marco Mastrodascio

Continuous Improvement Practice in Local Government
Insights from Australia and New Zealand
Matthew Pepper, Oriana Price and Arun Elias

For more information about this series, please visit: www.routledge.com/Routledge-Focus-on-Business-and-Management/book-series/FBM

Corporate Governance Models

A Critical Assessment

Marco Mastrodascio

Routledge
Taylor & Francis Group

NEW YORK AND LONDON

First published 2022
by Routledge
605 Third Avenue, New York, NY 10158

and by Routledge
2 Park Square, Milton Park, Abingdon, Oxon, OX14 4RN

*Routledge is an imprint of the Taylor & Francis Group, an
informa business*

Library of Congress Cataloguing-in-Publication Data
Names: Mastrodascio, Marco, author.
Title: Corporate governance models: a critical assessment /
Marco Mastrodascio.
Description: New York, NY: Routledge, 2022. | Series:
Routledge focus on business and management | Includes
bibliographical references and index.
Identifiers: LCCN 2021038037 (print) | LCCN 2021038038
(ebook) | ISBN 9781032126982 (hardback) | ISBN
9781032127019 (paperback) | ISBN 9781003225805 (ebook)
Subjects: LCSH: Corporate governance.
Classification: LCC HD2741.M338 2022 (print) | LCC HD2741
(ebook) | DDC 658.4--dc23
LC record available at https://lccn.loc.gov/2021038037
LC ebook record available at https://lccn.loc.gov/2021038038

ISBN: 978-1-032-12698-2 (hbk)
ISBN: 978-1-032-12701-9 (pbk)
ISBN: 978-1-003-22580-5 (ebk)

DOI: 10.4324/9781003225805

Typeset in Times New Roman
by MPS Limited, Dehradun

Contents

Preface

Corporate governance is defined as the set of economic and legal mechanisms through which organizations are governed (Denis and McConnell, 2003). By minimizing agency conflicts, Corporate governance allows suppliers of finance to earn a return on their investment, thereby contributing to long-term value creation (Shleifer and Vishny, 1997). However, to do so, corporate governance systems have to precisely define the rights, responsibilities and roles of all agents involved in the corporate governance process.

In the last two decades, multiple corporate scandals (e.g., Volkswagen, Lehman Brothers) have shown how current governance frameworks might be inadequate in the current business environment. Despite being designed to reduce agency conflicts, some governance frameworks have de facto encouraged opaque business practices. This has, in turn, generated a strong mistrust towards the current economic system. In response to these scandals, multiple regulations (e.g., SOX) were enacted to limit misbehaviour and improve firms' governance. Nonetheless, it is still unclear what defines good governance. The answer to this question is likely to vary across countries as each governance system is shaped by national factors, such as the level of capital market development or the degree of investor protection. In this respect, this book provides a comprehensive overview of each governance system (i.e., one-tier, two-tier and traditional models) by analysing their respective strengths and weaknesses. Furthermore, the authors provide several case studies that allow examining their practical implementation.

In my view, this book constitutes a valid first step towards bridging the gap between academic and professional views of corporate governance. Furthermore, I believe this book is timely. The current Covid-19 and climate crisis have emphasised the importance of resilience for corporations. Sound governance mechanisms can play a vital role in ensuring this. For example, a proxy fight has recently allowed a small hedge fund to install three directors on Exxon's board with the aim to address the company's environmental footprint. Finally, recent years were characterised by an increasing trend towards greater transparency. In this respect, good corporate governance can spur companies to increase their ESG and financial transparency, thereby helping to rebuild trust in the economic system.

References

Denis, D. K., and J. J. McConnell. 2003. International Corporate Governance. *Journal of Financial and Quantitative Analysis* 38 (1): 1–36.
Shleifer, A., and R. W. Vishny. 1997. A Survey of Corporate Governance. *Journal of Finance* 52 (2): 737–783.

Michele Pizzo
(Full professor of Business Administration
at the University of Campania 'Luigi Vanvitelli')

Acknowledgments

I have learnt in life that sometimes 'being strong' means getting help and support from people who we can count on especially in the darkest moments of our life when we do not have any hope and energy left to fight.

This book would not have been possible without the support of four people who have helped me when I needed them the most and did not leave me alone in the dark. These beautiful souls are D. Borg; V. Tomaso; J. Timpano; R. Lockery. I will never stop thanking you...

I would also like to thank my mentor Prof. Denita Cepiku who has always been an unlimited source of inspiration, perseverance and motivation.

Last but not least, to my dear friend Daniele who did not have a chance to see this accomplishment but I know that he is proud of me.

Thank you...

Introduction

The concept of corporate governance (CG) has been developed throughout the years becoming a topic of extensive interdisciplinary reflection such as legal scholarships, studies of pure and applied economics, management and business strategy disciplines. The reasons behind this interdisciplinary interest stem from the fact that corporations still remain the fundamental units of modern market capitalist nations. The organisational structure of these corporations, their functioning mechanisms, the sources of the financial resources available and, above all, the relationship among those who own, manage and control these resources are all necessary elements to fruitfully assess the impact of these organisations on the economic growth both at the national and global level.

Running a business requires the contribution of different subjects who cooperatively work in order to obtain an adequate remuneration for the efforts made. Ideally, organisations should be operating in a safe and friendly environment where loyal, trustworthy individuals share the same values, principles, scopes and same models of rationality. If this were the case, planning institutional assets, both proprietary and governance assets, would be rather straightforward as every single entity in the market would adopt the same model of loyalty and reasonableness with equivalent alternative institutional assets. According to this utopian economic world view, keeping the population's welfare unchanged would require the government to equally assign the production of goods and provision of services to organisations operating in a perfect competition system. Therefore, in a free-trade economic system, there would not be difference whether a manufacturing firm is structured as a Joint-stock company or as a Cooperative. In addition, the presence of representatives of workers, banks and local political communities would be irrelevant for the functioning of the board of directors and, nevertheless, the entire

DOI: 10.4324/9781003225805-101

economic system would be highly efficient due to the development of economic relations at no transaction cost. In the real world, neither perfect information nor rationality or homogeneous preference exist. A shrewd planning of proprietary and governance assets is therefore crucial to allow organisations and all economic systems to function productively.

The global situation has been hit in the last fifteen years by the financial crisis that occurred in 2007/2008 and the current COVID-19 pandemic. These negative crises have definitely created an imbalance, in terms of power exerted among the different players of the economic system, by increasing complexity, uncertainty and ambiguity due to asymmetric information and increasing lack of transparency. Consequently, the inadequate running of businesses has led to the loss of investors' money and trust in the economic system.

As the business scandals that occurred all over the world have undoubtedly revealed the inherent flows in contemporary CG practices. This obviously drew attention from public opinion especially in regard to the integrity and the attitude of firms towards both their shareholders and society, the number of CG structures available has risen worldwide in order to respond to the national differences in terms of historical, cultural and economic tradition. Based on a critical assessment of the different CG structures adopted at the international level, this book aims at finding, if existent, the most suitable model by analysing the economic, social and cultural factors that can influence the choice of a specific CG system. With no presumption or idea of completeness regarding the complex argument of CG, this book is divided into four chapters.

The first chapter covers all the diverse concepts of CG with a historical path that goes from the East Indian Company established in 1600 to what the CG system means in the third millennium. This chapter also analyses the concept of corporate social responsibility and the tools that are currently used to analyse the social impact of firms' operations. In the last part of the chapter, attention is paid to the issues arising from the separation between property and control within open corporations.

The second chapter of the book starts by analysing the peculiarities and the functioning mechanisms of the different systems of CG available nowadays. In the second part of the chapter, an investigation of the CG systems adopted by the main capitalist countries is performed. More specifically, the countries investigated are the United States, United Kingdom, Germany, France and Japan, and a brief introduction to the Italian context is provided even though it is extensively examined in chapter three. This comparative analysis aims at extrapolating the main endogenous and exogenous factors that can influence the choice to adopt a specific system of CG in the diverse countries analysed. This chapter concludes with the presentation of a few case studies in order to provide a pragmatic view of the analysed theme.

The third chapter, as briefly mentioned in chapter two, will specifically look at CG systems available and, above all, those mainly chosen by firms operating in the Italian territory. Particular attention will be paid to the effects caused by the reform of company law, entered into force on January 1, 2004, which, in fact, introduced two new systems of CG, the one-tier and two-tier systems, respectively. In addition, this chapter will also deal with the primary legislation source of voluntary adoption by companies, more specifically, the Italian Corporate Governance Code, the Preda's Code and other codes also used at the international level. Results will show that even though Italy is currently aligned with other countries in terms of CG systems available, the majority of organisations still favour the traditional model which is deeply rooted in the Italian corporate system.

The fourth chapter endeavours to provide a compelling answer to the following research question: *What is the best corporate governance system?* The answer provided is based on the analysis of the different CG models adopted both nationally and internationally and, above all, on the drawbacks induced by nominalism.

1 Origins and Definitions of Corporate Governance

1.1 Importance of the Corporate Governance Concept

Although the concept of CG[1] has become a major issue within the business world only in the past three decades, the word governance dates back to the fourteenth century. The word governance, from its Latin root 'gubernare,' is generally identified either as the action or method to wisely and responsively govern organisations (Cadbury, 2002). Since the Cicero's view of the role of governing according to which 'he that governs sits quietly at the stern and scarce is seen to stir,'[2] the concept of CG has been developed throughout the years becoming a topic of extensive interdisciplinary reflection such as legal scholarships, studies of pure and applied economics, management and business strategy disciplines. The reasons behind this interdisciplinary interest stem from the fact that corporations still remain the fundamental units of modern market capitalist nations. The organisational structure of these corporations, their functioning mechanisms, the sources of the financial resources available and, above all, the relationship among those who own, manage and control these resources are all necessary elements to fruitfully assess the impact of these organisation on the economic growth both at the national and global level. Within the relations established among these elements, an important role is played by the 'ownership structure' which is, in fact, able to drive power, rights and responsibilities within corporations (Colli, 2006). Consequently, the ownership structure of a firm is crucial for its ability to influence the level of performance and how resources are used at both microeconomic and macroeconomic levels.

The concept of *CG* It is known that the expression was defined for the first time by the Cadbury Report[3] as *the system by which companies are managed and controlled or, more generally, constitutes the set of rules, procedures and mechanisms that define the decision-making*

DOI: 10.4324/9781003225805-1

process at the highest corporate levels by giving, to a greater or lesser extent, the subjects involved a 'voice' in this process, in order to be able to protect their interests and investments.[4] Among its purposes, this set of rules has the effect of reducing the agency and transaction costs and favouring the alignment of possibly diverging interests and the reduction of existing information asymmetries.

The issues relating to the CG system of a company have been the subject of analysis by scholars for a long time, although the attention around the topic has grown significantly only in the last two decades. However, initially, only *blue chips* were the first to adopt CG rules, even the smallest companies, *mid or small caps*, decide to adopt them in order to access the capital market.

Overall, the importance of this theme has grown enormously in recent years basically due to the following three main reasons:

1   the increase of privatisations that have taken place around the world,[5] which averagely, this kind of operations, from 1990 to today, has generated for the countries that have carried out revenue from 2.7% to 27% of GDP. Privatisations have been conducted by following two roughly alternative approaches: favouring the creation of a widespread shareholder base in order to avoid the concentration of power (e.g. Apple in the USA) and supporting the creation of a batch of reference shareholders (e.g. Telecom Italia in Italy).

The intense privatisation process has definitely provoked some questions such as:

*   *Does the new public company need to implement new strategies and targets?*
*   *What role should the state play as a shareholder?*
*   *Can a corporate raider reach the control of a public company?*

The type of influence that the privatisation process exerts on CG depends not only on the severity of the rules, but also on the interpretation given to them and on the aims pursued by the political sphere, which plays a crucial role in the privatisation process, which is closely linked to the objectives that privatisation sets itself. In fact, the purposes of the privatisation are not only derived from what is sanctioned by the rules. The plentiful situations that the CG is called to face and the extent of the discretion that the political sphere has can vary the range of objectives and priorities pursued especially in the case of intensive privatisation process where companies operate in very different contexts while the surrounding conditions change significantly. The multiplicity of the purposes that privatisations aim to can be deduced from the extent of the privatisation process itself, which has affected a great variety of countries in recent decades, each of them characterised by different conditions and maturity of the economic, entrepreneurial, financial and legal system.

The purposes of the privatisation process, which has robustly influenced the adoption of CG systems by companies, can be categorised into three broad types of motivations:[6] ideological, functional and competitive.

From an ideological point of view, privatisations are the offspring of the great social and political evolution which, on a world level, has experienced the historical defeat of command or planned economies. The competition between market systems and centralised ones has seen the latter losing especially since market systems began to increasingly and consistently base their development on innovation.

From a functional point of view, the reasons for privatisation stem from the belief according to which economic activities carried out by government-owned companies usually deliver a lower levels of efficiency than those delivered by companies subjected to market discipline. The assumption is based, rather than on empirical evidence, on the logical impossibility of obtaining better results in the long term than those ensured by a correctly functioning market, which is presumably able to evaluate every single initiative and invest resources and knowledge most prolifically, thus allowing the growth of the most efficient operators and the elimination of inefficient ones. Based on these assumptions, the best that the government as an operator could aspire to obtain would be to imitate the market, but at that point, the usefulness of keeping the company in government hands would cease.

Finally, there is the competitive perspective which is the most influential reason leading to the privatisation of the largest government-owned enterprises, even where consolidated political beliefs and traditions of good bureaucratic efficiency seemed to presume the indefinite survival of the public control of some enterprises. Therefore, if the CG rules and the spirit through which those rules are followed within a country, it is likely that the operator that gives greater reliability to the market is the State with a large privatisation program and adequate technical skills to manage it.

2   the growing access to the financial market by small investors who are generally disinterested or poorly informed about the performance of the company they are investing.

This new type of investor represents an increasing part among the operators of the stock market, especially in Europe and the United States. Therefore, in joint-stock companies is relevant for two reasons:

- the greater diffusion of equity investments makes shareholders' protection a political problem;
- small shareholders generally have less skills than professional shareholders to monitor management behaviour, and therefore, have less 'voice' within the decision-making system as they rarely attend to shareholders' meetings, and when they are present they do not actively participate to the meeting.

3   the so-called corporate scandals which have highlighted how investor protection is often lacking.

In industrialised countries, the economic and financial crisis that occurred in 2007/2008, which followed the period of strong growth in the second half of the 1990s, was characterised by a series of cases that highlighted bad governance behaviours, such as *off-balance loans; self-dealing; communication of biased information to investors and insider trading; fraud.* The result of this misbehaviour was the loss of billions of dollars which, subsequently, destroyed companies and peoples' lives. Among the main corporate scandals which occurred worldwide, there are:

- Waste Management Inc. (over $1.7 billion in fake earnings);
- Enron Corporation (loss of over $74 billion as Enron's share price collapsed from around $90 to under $1 within a year);
- WorldCom (almost $11 billion);
- Tyco International (loss of over $150 million and inflation of $500 million in the company reports);
- Lehman Brothers (hidden over $50 billion in loans);
- Madoff Investment Security LLC (tricking investors out of over $64.8 billion);
- Ahold (inflated profits by $700 million);
- Parmalat and Cirio (€14 billion, which represents approximately 1% of the Italian GDP).

All these defaults "have shown that something was out-of-line with corporate governance, financial reporting and above all with auditing, at the end of the twentieth century" (Fera P., Pizzo M., Vinciguerra R., and Ricciardi G., 2021).

1.1.1 Definitions and Approaches to Corporate Governance

The change occurred in the dynamics of the capitalist system and the great wave of financial scandals that took place at the end of the last century and the beginning of the millennium, and have made CG become one of the most relevant issues in recent decades both academically and a practice/business level.

Corporate governance concerns the governance of companies and the management of relationships between the shareholders/owners of the company (the principals) and the management (the agents). More specifically, CG refers to the articulated system of relationships and interests between controlling shareholders of a company, investors (minority or outside shareholders) and the management structure of the company (Fiori & Tiscini, 2014).

Large corporations are now owned by a large number of shareholders who, on the one hand, have to delegate a small group of people to direct and manage the corporation and, on the other hand, implement an effective control system on their work.

Adam Smith in the *An Inquiry Into the Nature and Causes of the Wealth of Nations* (1776) pointed out that 'if whoever manages a business is a different person from the one who owns it, it is legitimate to suspect that managers, administering other people's money, do not put the same effort and care that they would put in administering their own.' Therefore, one of the main issues related to CG is the relationship between shareholders and the management.

However, the concept of CG goes far beyond the simple relationship between shareholders and managers. In fact, it involves whoever has an interest in the company such as lenders, employees, customers and suppliers. Therefore, there is the need to identify rules and practices of CG in order to guarantee the protection of the stakeholders' interests.

Overall, CG refers to the system of rules according to which companies are managed and controlled and this is the result of traditions, behaviours and rules elaborated by the single economic and juridical systems and it is certainly not attributable to a single model easily exported and imitated in all legal systems.

Despite the large number of contributions that have been produced on the CG over the last few decades, it should be noted that, to date, a shared definition of CG has not yet been reached. In general, definitions differ from each other in terms of extent and a variety of both stakeholders that are considered in the economic governance process (shareholders, managers, suppliers, employees, financial intermediaries, consumers) and for corporate bodies or mechanisms that

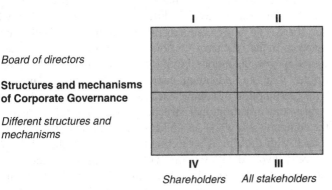

Figure 1.1 Conceptual structures of corporate governance.

are held responsible for the CG function (board of directors, auditing firm, top management, board of statutory auditors, etc.).

In regard to first aspect (extent and variety of stakeholders), CG ranges from definitions that consider the interests of shareholders and capital investors in general to be worthy of protection, to others in which it is argued that the activity of governance must balance the interests of all stakeholders.

In relation to the second aspect (authorities responsible for the control function), there are two extreme positions: those who believe that the body responsible for defining and resolving CG issues is mainly the board of directors and, oppose at those who are convinced that CG is a complex set of structures and rules aiming at composing different interests that converge into the company. In order to represent the different conceptual structures of CG, Figure 1.1 combines structures and mechanisms of CG and the interests considered in the CG process.

In the first quadrant, only the interest of the shareholders is considered as worthy of protection and the board of directors is the only authority proposed to perform the governance function. In the second quadrant, the interest of various categories of stakeholders is worthy of protection while the board of directors has the responsibility of carrying out the function of governance. In the third quadrant, the interest of all stakeholders has to be protected while the process of economic governance sees the operation of numerous elements internal and external to the company.

In the fourth quadrant, the interest of only shareholders is worthy of protection while the CG process is the result of the operation of numerous internal and external components

From the combinations of two elements considered (structure/mechanisms of CG and interests protected), different definitions of CG may arise. However, there is no single comprehensive definition of CG able to cover all the aspects. In fact, the term 'corporate governance' is susceptible to both broad and narrow definitions, but it is an important point that it is a concept, rather than an individual instrument (Narayana Murthy, 2003[7]). With no presumption of completeness, CG can be identified as a set of tools, rules and organisational structures that regulate the management of the company as a whole, established internally or externally to the company itself with the aim of protecting the interests of the subjects directly or indirectly involved with the events of the business and reconcile those that may conflict with each other. After this brief classification that concerns the various classes of definitions relating to CG, two important conceptions are presented: the narrow and enlarged concept of CG.

1.1.1.1 Narrow Concept of Corporate Governance

The narrow concept of CG is strongly influenced by the models adopted in Anglo-Saxon capitalist systems, where large corporations are characterised by a pulverised ownership structure so-called public company. Shareholders are, in fact, the category of stakeholders who have the right of control. This right is exercised by expressing their vote on some important decisions and appointing the members of the board of directors and being owners, they have a strong interest in maximising efficiency and wealth produced in the long run. In this scenario, CG is seen as the tool through which managers are incentivized to pursue the interests of shareholders and the relationship between shareholders and members of the board of directors can be configured as an agency relationship. According to the restricted concept of CG, the right and duty to govern the company belongs only to those who own shares of risk capital. However, those who govern the company must pay great attention to the stakeholders providing blurred contributions to the final business result, which is difficult to obtain *ex ante* and verify *ex post*. However, while some contributions from stakeholders can be easily replaced and found in the market, other contributions that involve scarce resources and skills can seriously damage the company if lost. In fact, company performance is influenced by the behaviour of stakeholders who make crucial contributions to their survival and for this reason, they pay attention to meeting their expectations.

Within this concept of CG, the main problem occurs when the shareholding structure is divided so as to give rise to the phenomenon of the separation of ownership of risk capital shares from the control of the company, intended such as the right to make major economic governance decisions.[8] More specifically, the excessive splitting of the shareholding structure determines two significant consequences: reduces the incentive of shareholders to carry out adequate control over the work of executives and gives managers control of the board of directors and, in fact, of the company as a whole. The resulting phenomenon of *free riding* tends to manifest itself because no shareholder possesses sufficient shares of capital, therefore, a sufficient percentage of the residual return of the company, to justify the costs associated with the definition of contracts with other stakeholders and to check compliance with the terms set out therein. At these conditions, managers and members of the board of directors can make decisions that are aimed at maximising their own interests to the detriment of the interests of shareholders and corporate efficiency.

However, the legislation should not regulate in too much details the methods of CG, but it ought to create the institutional mechanisms capable of protecting the interests of minority stakeholders.

The regulatory indications issued by various national and international bodies are all aimed, at least on paper, at the goal of increasing the accountability of managers and the autonomy of the board of directors through, for example, increasing the number of independent external directors; creating committees with specific tasks composed mainly or exclusively of independent directors; separating of the role of chief executive officer and chairman; timely delivering of information regarding the board meeting and periodically evaluating the work of the directors.

1.1.1.2 Enlarged Concept of Corporate Governance

The enlarged concept of CG overcomes the limits of the narrow concept by extending its attention to all the stakeholders of the company and considering the internal and external of the company that influences the governance process.

More specifically, the enlarged concept takes into account the fact that the separation between ownership and control occurs only in the cases of listed and large companies.

From this consideration, companies cannot pursue the only purpose of increasing the share value but must also be able to have to meet the expectations of various stakeholders, such as clients, suppliers, employees and creditors of which interests must be considered as important as that of the shareholders who, in fact, take risk.

The extant research conducted on the enlarged concept of CG has highlighted that the issue related to the separation of ownership and control is specific to large Anglo-Saxon public companies. In addition, companies cannot limit themselves to pursuing the satisfaction of shareholders' interests and maximising shareholder value, but must meet the expectations of numerous stakeholders. An important role must be played by the national legislation, which helps define the balance of power between various stakeholders within a company.

In conclusion, each CG model is composed of a large number of interdependent variables, which are the results of the slow process of evolution of the institutions that regulate the behaviour and values of people who live and operate within a given geographical context.

Strictly linked to the two abovementioned concepts of CG, two different approaches can be identified: *shareholders' value approach* and *stakeholders' value approach*. Based on the main principle according to which a CG system should be able to create value, these approaches consider two actors, of which interest should be protected and guaranteed by the company.

1.1.1.3 Shareholders' Value Approach

According to the *Shareholders' Value approach*, CG is aimed at defining rules and incentives so that the behaviour of management coincides with the interests of the shareholders due to the fact that the latter are the only ones who bear the full risk of seeing their capital invested in the company destroyed by an erroneous decisions taken by the management and, at the same time, being (unlike customers and creditors) by any form of contract (Rappaport, 1986).

According to this approach, only the interests of one specific group of actors in the corporate system is considered relevant: the shareholders. Consequently, the ultimate goal of the company is that of fully meeting the expectation of the shareholders in terms of value creation which, consequently, will lead to create value for all stakeholders as well. The shareholders' approach is based on the assumption according to which creating value for all shareholders would measure the value created for shareholders impossible for the board of directors and also their activities would be challenging to control.

However, regardless of the type of approach chosen, decisions and actions are always aimed at maximising personal benefit for all the actors involved. The decision maker will always maximise his/her personal benefit, therefore, in the principal (shareholders) – agent (management) relationship, the latter will always be incentivised to take decisions that will eventually benefit him/herself at the principal's expenses (*agency problem*). In addition, the principal cannot control the agent's activities *ex-ante* and this makes the opportunistic behaviour of the agent easier to adopt and harder to detect. Therefore, without adequate countermeasures aimed at preserving the interests of the company owners, the opportunistic behaviour of the agent, in the shareholder-value approach, is certain.

Businesses must be managed in a way that generates money and therefore adds value for their owners especially because they are the only category of stakeholders who, unlike the others, are remunerated on a residual basis. In fact, in exchange for the capital conferred on the company, shareholders obtain shares that give them the right to receive a certain percentage of the income that the company achieves after having paid all the other suppliers of production factors. If then, in a financial year, this result is negative, they bear the *pro-quota* loss that the company has suffered. In summary, by accepting to be remunerated on a residual basis, shareholders bear the risk of the company and allow other stakeholders to receive a periodic and contractually established remuneration.

1.1.1.4 Stakeholders' Value Approach

The stakeholders' value approach starts from the assumption that the ultimate goal of a company is to create value for whoever has an interest in the company. For this reason, it would be necessary to grant all those who supply strategic inputs to the company (e.g. employees) the right to participate and influence the business' activities. More specifically, companies, for the concrete realisation of economic activity, require the contribution of numerous stakeholders: the contributors of risk capital, the contributors of loan capital, suppliers of raw materials and services, workers, customers, the state, the local community, etc.

However, this assumption evidently contains an unrealistic simplification due to the fact that an approach that is too broad that considers a large number of corporate actors is not usable and therefore useless. In addition, corporate objectives and strategies are the results of a process of interaction between people and institutions who are interested not so much (or not only) in achieving better overall performance of the company, but in obtaining the largest portion of the result for themselves.

Therefore, based on the conception of business as an 'open system,' the supporters of this approach define that this system must be able to create value for all those who have interests in the company.

These subjects, with specific interests, act within a larger system, the local community, which provides the regulatory and economic infrastructures necessary for the conduct of business activities.

These activities represent the result of the involvement of numerous subjects who provide resources (tangible or intangible, monetary or non-monetary) for the company and, therefore, bear the risk of a negative result produced by the company. These stakeholders have *de jure* or *de facto* drawn up 'contracts' with the company in which each category offers a specific good or service in order to obtain adequate remuneration.

The total value created therefore consists of not only the return on equity (through dividends and capital gains), but also the salary paid to employees (human capital), the interest conferred on creditors, taxes and fees paid to the government and the local community which give to the company the ability to operate.

Table 1.1 shows the main features, strengths and weaknesses of the two approaches analysed.

Overall, regardless of the approach taken, the opportunistic behaviour is a constant due to the fact that each actor that plays a role in the company selfishly aims to maximise his/her own benefit. The

Table 1.1 Shareholders' and Stakeholders' approach to value creation

	Shareholders' Approach	Stakeholders' Approach
Features	The purpose is the maximisation of shareholders' wealth through productive, allocative and dynamic efficiency. The measurement parameter is the market value.	The company must be a socially responsible entity that pursues the interests of all stakeholders.
Advantages	Market value is a measurable goal. As the market value increases, the *stakeholders* (non-shareholders) will also benefit from it.	*Stakeholders* are more incentivized to create value in the long run.
Disadvantages	Management takes advantage of information asymmetries, which makes its actions partly undetectable and unquestionable. Agency problems can lead to an underinvestment while pursuing short-term performance can hinder long-term projects.	There is a lack of distinct purposes. The *principal-agent problem* can be worsened by the fact that numerous interests (of all stakeholders) are involved and very hard to satisfy all.

company, on other hand, has to reduce this opportunism by trying to align, at a different extent, its interest with that of the various stakeholders involved in the value creation process.

1.2 The Separation Between Ownership and Control

The dimensional growth of companies is inevitably linked to their availability of capital. As long as the size remains small, the capital invested by an individual owner (entrepreneur) and the loans obtained from banks are able to meet the investment needs of the company.

However, the increase in company size must be suitably aligned with an adequate balance between loan capital and shareholders' equity. The increase in loans must find a fair counterweight in the capital owned, which depends on the risks assumed, in order to guarantee adequate financial flexibility which is necessary for the company to adapt to the changing environment.

The company growth is the result of the increase in the *number of shareholders* (e.g. through the listing on the stock exchange) as well as the change in the *legal structure* (e.g. transition from partnership to the joint-stock company) and *organisational structure* (from functional to multidivisional structure).

In classical business theory, the focus was only on the entrepreneur while the manager was placed only on the side of the entire system. Moreover, the company owner, as a provider of stock capital, and the entrepreneur, as a business leader, were the same person who beared the full risk and gained the whole profit.

On the contrary, the empirical analysis conducted by Berle and Means (1932) redefines a new company perspective. The innovative aspect of their work relies on the identification and analysis of the separation of the position of owner (shareholders) of the company from the position of the manager. According to the Berle and Means, between these two corporate actors, managers play a dominant role of insiders which is indirectly given to managers from the pulverised shareholding, typical of large companies (La Porta, Lopez-de-Silanes, Shleifer, & Vishny, 2000).

Contrary to what would be expected today, Berle and Means did not, however, conclude according to which it is necessary to find mechanisms to force management to act in the interests of shareholder. Berle and Means claim that through the independence of the management from the shareholders, the latter no longer acts as mere agents of the shareholders but pursues the interests of the entire company (Dcmsetz, 1983) instead as being led from social responsibility.

In the modern literature, Berle and Means' basic theory of the separation between shareholders and management is widely recognised as valid; in terms of regulatory policy, however, the conclusions are not widely shared.

1.2.1 Open Corporation

The separation between ownership and control is a specific feature of the *open corporation* which is a corporate structure, widespread in both the United Kingdom and the United States, characterised by shares listed and available for exchange on public market shares are still available for public trading. According to Wagner (1991), open corporation was developed in order to allow companies to sustain rapid growth by keeping on innovating especially when the company starts aging (Peters, 1990).

However, the constant expansion of the shareholding structure due to the public offerings of shares on the stock exchange (flotations) has made corporation owners (shareholders) powerless and unable to control managers' activities. On the other hand, this system has enabled companies to implement restless expansion especially due to the activities performed by professionally and technically trained managers who led to an epochal change in management techniques and a consequent gain in efficiency compared to small-sized family-run companies.

In addition, Berle and Means describe a corporation owned by numerous shareholders who do not bear the full risk like in a concentrated shareholder company, where it is possible that all the family savings are in fact invested in the business. Therefore, shareholders–managers will tend to be particularly conservative and prudent and *a priori* will exclude particularly risky projects, even if they are harbingers of high expected returns in case of success.

In contrast, Berle–Means' corporation shareholders typically own very diversified portfolios. On the one hand, this circumstance weakens their influence on the management of each company, on the other hand, it protects them from any prejudicial events of one of the investments they have in their portfolio. Therefore, managers will be incentivized to take on higher risks, especially to the extent that their remuneration includes a variable component directly related to the performance of their investments.

The Berle–Means' open corporation which is still the prevailing corporation form in both the United States and the United Kingdom1 has some drawbacks as well. The latter were identified and formally defined for the first time in the years by Jensen and Meckling (1976) with the concept of *agency problems,* which is detailed in the next paragraph with the most important issues related to the open corporation.

1.2.1.1 The Agency Problem

According to Coase (1937), an agency relationship occurs when one or more people (principals) delegate the performance of other activities to others (agents). Theoretically, managers (agents) should operate in the interests of the shareholders (principals) in order to maximise the value of their investment (the shareholders' value). However, things do not always go this way, and this is because often managers, aware of the limited possibilities of control available to their principals, have different targets and this can lead them to adopt behaviours oriented to their own interest to the detriment of that of shareholders.

However, the difference in purposes between agent and principal is necessary but not sufficient condition for an agency problem to arise. In fact, the impossibility of drawing up contracts able to predict any possible future situations, the costs associated with monitoring the opportunistic agent are all conditions favouring the agency problem.

It can be identified by two main drivers of the agency problems: conflicts of interest and information asymmetry.

The conflict of interest between managers and shareholders stems from the distribution of the power within the open corporation. More specifically, shareholders are external to the company and holders of all (or almost) of the residual rights[9] (Fama & Jensen, 1983), while the management is internal to the company and has only a small portion of it. However, as a decision-maker within the company, the manager has, unlike the external shareholder, many possibilities to meet their needs alternatively. In fact, there are many ways to increase managers' benefits, such as an increase in notoriety and prestige, better career opportunities, status, higher salaries and less work or less likelihood of layoffs. All these rewards can be obtained through the company growth which will depend on the decisions taken by the manager who, in order to maximise his/her own benefits, will inevitably make decisions of at the expense of external shareholders or, in any case, riskier than decisions that would be taken in case it was the sole shareholder and therefore had to bear the entire cost of the decisions taken. There are many formal demonstrations of the existence of a conflict of interest between management and shareholders. For instance, Figure 1.2 shows graphically the contribution to the market value of a company of additional employees within a profit function. This is the

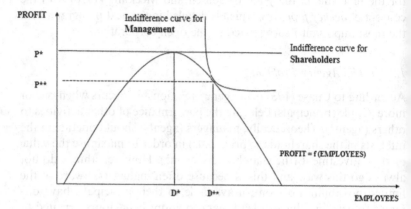

Figure 1.2 Contribution to market value creation of additional employees.

typical case where management inflates corporate staff functions at the expense of shareholders.

The profit function shows the optimal number of collaborators whose exceeding or non-achievement involves a reduction in profits. It is assumed that this function runs parallel to the abscissa axis due to the fact that the shareholders have only residual rights and therefore are only interested in maximising the company result. Therefore, shareholders prefer point P* to P**.

Additional employees will have for the management, unlike the shareholder, a particular personal value, for instance, represented by the opportunity to reduce the negative effects of his/her activities or increase the amount of free time. Therefore, the management will no longer be interested only in the value of the residual result and this is shown by indifference curves no longer run parallel to the abscissa axis and different from those of the shareholders.

The subjective value of the additional collaborators will fall within the utility function of the management. The manager will therefore prefer the point P**, D**, data P*> P** and D* <D**, thus opting for more employees and less profit. From the shareholders' point of view, it will therefore be a second-best solution.

As a result of this explanation, a question arises: Why do shareholders have to bear entire costs for services consumed by the management? The answer to this question refers to the asymmetric disposal of information between the management and shareholders (information asymmetry).

Managers (as insiders) are able to estimate the (true) profit function of the company than shareholders outside the company as the former has better quality information than shareholders who, in open corporations, hold a small portion of shares and the cost-benefit calculation for the reduction of systemic information asymmetries appears not very advantageous to them. In fact, shareholders have to bear the costs for understanding and evaluating the decisions and actions taken by while the resulting economic benefits will benefit all shareholders. Therefore, shareholders are discouraged to bear the cost of informing themselves regarding the management activity.

In conclusion, shareholders are unable to monitor the activities of the management within an open corporation. In Figure 1.2, the gap P* – P** is therefore to be considered as an agency cost in a world where information is distributed unevenly. The agency cost is the 'price' that shareholders have to pay for the benefits of employing a specialised management.

The consequence of the conflict of interest and information asymmetry is a margin of discretion, within which the owners are confronted with uncertainty in relation to the actions of management. The final purpose of the shareholders is to reduce this discretionary gap as much as possible.

The geographical context where the corporation operates is able to influence the type of methods employed in order to reduce the agency problem. While in the United States and United Kingdom, characterised by the presence of the common law system, the control on managers stems from the market while in Europe and the control is exerted by institutions and regulations through the contract system (Porta et al. 1998). Even though in the literature the two schools of thought try to support the relative superiority of one or the other control methodology, in practice, defining a perfect method is not possible because none of these methods is exempt from criticism or unresolved questions. Moreover, in any developed economic system, institutional and market-based control never exist separately but are combined in order to exert an efficient control on the management.

Among the different control tools available to control the management, there are:

- *incentive contracts* which aim at minimising the conflict of interest by reducing *ex ante* the discretional gap between managers and shareholders that will be monitored *ex post*. For this reason, incentive contracts are considered the most efficient tool to reduce the agency problem. However, the usage of incentive contracts is necessary in case drafting the so-called *complete contract*[10]

(Besanko, Dranove, Shanley, & Schaefer, 2004) is impossible. Two types of incentive contracts can be identified:

1   explicit incentive contracts that are used in case of asymmetry information among the contracting party which can be enforced through an outside third-party (e.g. an arbitrator);
2   implicit incentive contracts that are used in case the management performance cannot be measured. The alignment between management and shareholders' interests and the inability to measure management performance requires the usage of incentive contracts that are carried out through various forms of participation in the result and capital. Among these forms of participation, the following forms of incentives are based on share prices: stock options, stock appreciation rights and stock grants.

Stock options are incentive tools extended to top management and members of the board of directors of a company or employees. More specifically, these tools assign the employee or manager the right to purchase shares (previously issued) or to subscribe new shares (newly issued).

The manager or employee who receives the offer of options, generally at an exercise price equal to or lower than the market price, has the opportunity to realise a capital gain if the share price exceeds exercise at a time subsequent to the granting of the options. Otherwise, the options lose its entire value. In an initial phase called *granting,* the company grants its employees and/or managers the right to purchase a certain number of shares in a predetermined future time frame and at a predetermined price. In a second phase called vesting, managers or employees assess the possibility to exercise the option granted. The final phase of *exercising* is the phase when the option right is actually exercised. Since the higher the price of the shares on which the option is based the higher is gain for the manager, from the incentive point of view, it is assumed that the granting of stock options stimulates management and employees to increase company value. This results in a reduction in the agency problem. However, it should not be thought that stock options have only positive effects on managers' behaviours. In fact, problems arise due to the existence of a different risk aversion between shareholders and management. In fact, an option plan represents only a potential profit for management and not a potential loss. Therefore, such an incentive model can generate in managers either a greater propensity for risk in management or behave from a short-term perspective or, unfortunately, in an irregular manner by falsifying data and results[11]. Additional negative aspects of the stock options are represented by the fact that the performance reached by the individual is not measurable and that all collaborators benefit from rising stock market prices and the stock market prices can decrease regardless of managers' actions.

Stock appreciation rights (SAR) are granted to employees as an alternative to stock options. The difference with stock options lies in the fact that, when the right is exercised, the difference between the value of the stock exchange price and the exercise price is paid directly by the company in cash (Haid, 1997). The positive results that can be obtained are the reduction of transaction costs, the reduction of the effect of the dilution of rights and the possibility of avoiding an outlay of the exercise price. Stock appreciation rights can therefore be considered virtual stock options, in fact, they have the same downsides as the stock options.

Stock grants represent the third method usually used to align the interest of shareholders with that of the management. It consists of granting equity to either the management or employees as part of their compensation. Therefore, employees and management are thus forced to be shareholders of the company for a determined period of time and, therefore, stimulate their interest in increasing the stock market value of the shares. Like the stock options and SAR, this method of participation aims at limiting the conflict of interest between shareholders and managers, however, it has the same drawbacks as the stock options and SAR.

- *markets* that are considered the most effective deterrents against the abuse by managers of the discretionary spaces available to them due to the information asymmetries with shareholders. More specifically, this control method is based on the assumption according to which the stock market price fully reflects the value of management performance. However, there are other factors that influence the stock price and, more generally the performance of the company, such as an efficient regulation of the stock market (against fraudulent behaviours such as insider trading[12]), and economic, political, social and psychological factors in the short run.

There are four main market control methods: the market for corporate control, the capital market, labour market for managers and products competition.

1   The literature on market for corporate control is based on the principle according to which poor management performance leads shareholders to leave the company by selling their equity and, therefore, it will cause a drop in the company's stock market value and, on other hand, an opportunity for the so-called raiders to acquire majority stakes in order to obtain profits. After obtaining control, the raiders will be able to layoff the management responsible for the misallocation of resources, eliminate unproductive members (in case of business group), introduce new CG forms better able to control the management. There are many drawbacks related to the market for corporate control such as the ability of managers to condition the legal system to make for a so-called *rent-seeking* (Tullock, 1993) more difficult to take place and implement defensive strategies by conditioning the structure of the company or contractual relations to reduce its market value or to force the raiders to review their objectives. Among these defensive strategies there are:

- Pac-man defence, when the target firm then tries to buy a majority stake in the company that has made a hostile takeover attempt (Gorzala, 2010);
- White Knight though which company looks itself for a more appropriate buyer which can be either a 'friendly' company or even your bank. The white knight aims at raising stock in the public causing share prices to rise (Ravenscraft & Scherer, 1987);
- Poison pills through which the company has, for example, granted particular rights to purchase shares or the possibility of exchanging bonds for shares or cash (poison debt) in the event of an acquisition (Heron & Lie, 2006);
- Staggered board according to which the management can only be partially replaced and that qualified majority shares are required for the replacements (Amihud & Stoyanov, 2017);
- Golden parachutes through which management is granted a substantial compensation in the event of a dismissal (Fich, Tran, & Walkling, 2013);
- Crown jewels which represents the sale of the most interesting company's activities to the raider (Lin, Ji, He, & Zhu, 2012);
- Merging and acquisition activities aimed at changing the structure of the company, so that it becomes too large to be incorporated or too expensive for the operation to be financed (DePamphilis, 2010);

- Greenmailing, which describes the situation in which the company repurchases its shares from those who took over.

In addition to the tools available for managers to avoid raiders' control of the company, two other factors cast doubt on the effective functionality of the market for corporate control: the free-riding problem and the positive external effects of the takeover bid.

According to *free-rider problem* theory Grossman and Hart (1980), small shareholders (Kandel, Massa, & Simonov, 2011) of an open corporation have a tendency to refuse to accept an offer which will deprive them of future income. Theoretically, if all small shareholders (owning a small number of shares) behaved according to this line of reasoning they could put the functionality of the market in crisis. However, there are strong doubts regarding the fact that the minority shareholders collectively carry out the type of reasoning set out. In fact, small shareholders, doubting the qualities of the new management, may decide to sell instead.

Regarding the positive effects of the takeover bid, the economic literature considers the fact that any offer to purchase made by the raider on the market, he/she implicitly declares that he/she has identified an interesting prey (target corporation). It follows that after the first offer, further competitors may be stimulated to carry out new offers which indirectly makes the costs for the search and selection of 'prey' higher. The result of this positive external effect is therefore to discourage potential raiders from making bids to the public.

2   The control mechanism by means of the capital market is based on the principle according to which each company aims at keeping low costs of capital and this implies that companies with bad performances are disadvantaged in raising capital. Consequently, poorly performing companies will have reduced financial resources compared to high performing competitors.

According to the control mechanism carried out by the capital market, a company with bad performances will therefore be characterised by a low valuation of its securities in the primary stock market with a low valuation of the securities, while in the bond market, the bad performance will be combined with a worse rating and worse conditions of issue. However, this type of control only works in case of the company actually forced to source liquidity from outside. Indeed, if companies are able to finance themselves through undistributed profits, this type of control cannot take place. The disciplining effect of the capital market would disappear 'in organisations that generate large cash flows but have low growth prospects' (Jensen, 1986: 324). The fact that shareholders are deprived of the opportunity to sanction the management is defined as 'agency cost of free cash flow' (Jensen, 1986).

The existence of this type of control is also known to managers who actually use external financing only when the company's internal cash flows are no longer available (Chen & Chen, 2011; Myers & Majluf, 1984).

3   The approach of reducing agency problems by means of the labour market considers that managers produce signals relating to their abilities by means of company results. According to this approach, these signals would be necessary for management as they allow it to create a reputation on the job market; and this is important since every member of the management is constantly confronted with a probability of being fired. In fact, bad business results, scandals or even the bankruptcy of the company, would heavily damage the reputation of a CEO on the job market and, consequently, it would severely limit his/her job options outside the company (Fama, 1980; Tuggle, 2010).

Reputation would then solve all agency problems between management and shareholders, allowing the management to have good options on the job market and to obtain salary increases from their company. Managers are therefore expected to be motivated to increase corporate value. However, there are many cases where executives and members of top management coming from poorly performing companies have found new rewarding jobs. In fact, this would suggest that personality, training, curriculum and working methodology are more important factors in the choice of a manager than the results of the previous employing company.

4   The fourth approach for agency problem reduction is based on the products competition. More specifically, the theory behind management control through competition in product markets argues that the stronger the competition, the lower the price-cost margins of the products of poorly managed companies will be (Hart, 1983). Unsatisfying company results would therefore allow management to be reprimanded by shareholders and forced to endure their methods and solutions to the low performance which, consequently, negatively affects the valuation of the company on both capital and labour market for managers. Therefore, competition in

products market can only indirectly lead to agency-problem control as it is considered only a necessary element to activate the other forms of market control previously outlined.

However, critique of this type of management control is based on the fact that companies with highly committed managers can still produce and sell products but are not able to have cash flow due to the unpredictability of market trends. In that case, managers would be faultlessly reprimanded and shareholders would get nothing in return. In addition, if there is low cash flow and, at the same time, profits hidden from shareholders and obtained by circumventing market limitations, the management misbehaviour must be proved. Therefore, a benchmark on the business results obtained by competitors could be, in fact, a potential solution to unmask managers producing with too reduced price-cost margin.

- *institutions* that transforms the relation between principal and gent in *a principal–supervisor–agent* relationship. There are three main types of institutional control over the management: shareholders' meeting, board of directors and external auditors.

  1 During shareholders' meetings, the highest corporate bodies such as the board of directors provide a report on the company's activities. The existence of the shareholders' meeting limits the agency problem *per se* as the management and the highest corporate bodies are accountable for the business operations carried out. In this sense, the correct convocation, organisation and the running of the shareholders' meetings is particularly relevant. In addition, some specific transactions require the approval of the majority in the shareholders' meeting (plenum meeting) which highlights the importance of the supervisory function.

However, in order that shareholders assess management's activity, they must obtain economic benefits in return in order to justify the costs beared and the efforts made to obtain knowledge and information necessary to perform the control. In fact, shareholders will calculate the opportunity cost (Spiller, 2011) in order to decide to whether evaluate or not the management' activity bearing, at the same time, the risk that the assessment will eventually benefit all shareholders. Therefore, only a person with a large number of shares would be willing to carry out this kind of research and assessment as she/he obtains benefits for a large number of shares.

1   Besides shareholders, the control of the management can be exerted by the board of directors, members of which are usually nominated by the shareholders.[13] The board of directors is able to limit the agency problem between managers and shareholders as the directors are less than shareholders but more specialised and are in more direct contact with the management. In fact, the main task of the board of directors is to control the pursuit of the shareholders' interests and, possibly, of other stakeholders,' implemented by the management. In the event that expectations are not met, the board of directors is expected to dismiss the management.

The problems arising from the introduction of the board of directors may be different depending on whether there is or not a majority shareholder.

In case there is a majority shareholder, there are two alternatives. First, the management pursues personal purposes by evading the control of the board of directors or in collusion with it; and second, the management in collusion with the board of directors unjustifiably penalises minority shareholders.

In case there is not a shareholder majority, there is only the possibility that the management evades the control of the board of directors or that it acts directly in collusion with it.

Overall, the main problem occurs when the representatives of the shareholders within the board of directors do not carry out efficient control over the management. This may be due to the fact that directors may obtain illicit profits in collusion with management or to the fact directors are often in direct and personal contact with members of top management and, therefore, tend to avoid conflicts.

A further issue is represented by the fact that 'many directors are unable or unwilling to devote the time and energy necessary to oversee the operation of the company, or to make financial commitment to its success' (Monks & Minow, 2001: 171).

In the case of open corporations where no majority shareholders can elect representatives on the board of directors, carrying out the control over the management is even more difficult as the directors' appointment, salary and information depends, in fact, on the decisions taken by the management. Due to the high number of possible issues, most of the best practice codes focus almost exclusively on the board of directors, defining its composition, size, committees, meeting methods, independence, presidency and many other aspects. However, as any other regulations can generate dysfunctional side effects depending on where the regulations are applied in terms of legal context, there are different codes.

2 The financial scandals[14] that occurred worldwide clearly demonstrated the insufficiency of management control only based on the activities performed by the shareholders' meeting and board of directors. External auditors can definitely limit management's freedom due to the fact that unlike the activities carried out by the board of directors, those undertaken by external auditors are precisely defined by law with no margin of discretion. However, a wrong or too risky company policy that is not against the law, cannot be contested by the auditors and this severely limits the effectiveness of the external auditor's action as a control body. In regard to large companies, this problem is even more difficult to solve, considering that only over time do auditors acquire the specific know-how in relation to large companies. For this reason, some codes of best practice issue recommendations also in relation to the composition and election of external auditors.

• the *Blockholders:* as explained in paragraph 1.2.1, big corporations are characterised by a widespread shareholding, and shareholders have no incentive to control the management due to the fact that the improvement in company performance that derives from the control activity benefits all of the shareholders and not just the shareholders performing the control activity. This is defined as free-rider problem (Grossman & Hart, 1980).

Control activity is expensive for those who exercise it, therefore shareholders who own a small portion of share capital do not normally carry out the activity hoping to benefit from the supervision exerted by other shareholders, usually large shareholders. In fact, according to the Blockholder theory, an improvement in performance can only occur 'by parties who already own a large share of the firm' (Shleifer & Vishny, 1986) and, therefore, are willing to bear the costs.[15]

Three main Blockholders can be identified:

• Cross-holdings: it is a situation when a corporation owns numerous stocks in another publicly traded company. In case of a large quantity of stocks, this category of shareholding becomes the so-called *Blockholder*. Therefore, the management of the controlled company have to follow the instructions given by the management of the Blockholder. If the management of the Blockholder company is not interested in the controlled company, the management of the latter will not be subjected to a strict control. In this case, the control exerted on the management of the controlled company is not effective.

On the other hand, one of the situations in which cross-holdings can be problematic is when companies hold stocks of each other, creating the so-called interlocks. In this case, there is the possibility for the management of several companies to start collusive relationships in order to mutually 'negotiate' a mild supervision or, in the worst-case scenario, to damage all the minority shareholders in the whole structure called pyramid structure.

The law, stock exchange regulations and codes of best practice require the top management and board members to communicate their interests to the market.

• Investment and retirement funds: characteristic of investment funds and pension funds is that of having significant shareholdings in non-financial companies among their investments.

In case of investors are dissatisfied with returns they can sell their assets which are therefore no longer controlled by the fund. Consequently, the discretionary powers of the fund management are significantly reduced. Investment funds are therefore expected to behave actively in controlling the management of the companies in which the funds have invested;

• Banks: the bank management is at least partially controlled by customer deposits and will therefore be responsible for supervising the work of companies whose profits are the foundation of the bank income. Despite the incentives for control activities mentioned, it cannot be denied that the link between banks and companies can also create problems. First of all, banks have the possibility of financing themselves in an alternative way to customers' deposits. In addition, there is the possibility of collusion between the management of the companies over which the bank exercises control and the bank management. In fact, company top management has at its disposal a multitude of ways to corrupt the management of the bank in order to limit or neglect the control and supervision activities such as the granting of better credit coverage and accepting unfavourable credit conditions.

• *Debt:* the last method of control on the management activities is represented by issues of bonds by companies that need to finance business expansion projects or maintain ongoing operations. Bonds are either issued on the primary market, which rolls out new debt, or on the secondary market, in which investors may purchase existing debt via brokers or other third parties. Overall, bonds are less volatile and more conservative than stock, however, have lower expected returns.

The control by means of debt does not depend on the fact that the company is externally financed but on the effect that the debt, once assumed, has on the management behaviour.

Jensen (1986) states that a promise of payment of dividends by the management is weak because they will always reduce the promised payments. Debts, on the other hand, allow management to be tied to its promise not to consume future cash flows for private purposes. Therefore, the presence of debt reduces the agency cost of free cash flows by reducing the portion of cash flow that management can dispose of at its discretion.

Debt is therefore an efficient method of control through which investors 'assure themselves of getting a return on their investment' (Shleifer & Vishny, 1997: 737). More specifically, the fear that the non-payment of bond debts may induce creditors to request the opening of a bankruptcy procedure therefore induces the management to make the payments due.

However, as the cases relating to Parmalat and Argentine bonds have taught us, the fear of non-payment of bond debts that can induce creditors to request the opening of a bankruptcy procedure does not seem to have had a decisive impact on the management and the result, unfortunately, it was that thousands of people saw their life savings fade away.

1.3 The Guiding Principles of Corporate Governance

According to the Cadbury report, released in 1991 in the United Kingdom, 'Corporate governance is the system by which businesses are directed and controlled.'[16] Therefore, CG can be identified as the main driver for reaching the integrity and efficiency within a company. Poor CG, on the other hand, can lead to weaken company's potential, and therefore, to financial difficulties and long-term damage to a company's reputation. The guiding principles that an effective and efficient system of CG should be able to apply in order to outperform other companies and attract investors, whose support can help to finance further growth, belong to distinct four categories: *account-ability, responsibility; fairness* and *transparency.*

Although the scope and meaning of 'accountability' have been extended in a number of directions, it principally refers to the monitoring, evaluation, and control of organisational agents to ensure that they behave in the interests of the stakeholders. Therefore, the accountability system includes monitoring, evaluating and controlling of the activities carried out by whoever entitled to manage the company so that every stakeholder's interest is satisfied (Mulgan, 2000). In applying the accountability principle, a central role is played by the board of directors that should present a balanced and understandable assessment of the company's position and prospects; specify the nature and extent of the significant risks it is willing to take; maintain sound risk management and internal control systems; establish formal and transparent arrangements for corporate reporting and risk management and for maintaining an appropriate relationship with the company's auditor; communicate with stakeholders at regular intervals, a fair, balanced and understandable assessment of how the company is achieving its business purpose (Vagadia, 2014). In conclusion, corporate accountability refers to ethical obligation of providing a reasonable explanation for the company's actions and conduct.

The second guiding principle of CG refers to responsibility which is strictly linked with the accountability principle. More specifically, the board of directors should be made accountable to the shareholders in regard to how the company has carried out its responsibilities. Shareholders give authority and power to the board of directors to act on behalf and in the best interests of the company. The board of directors, on the other hand, are responsible for overseeing the management of the business, appointing the chief executive and monitoring the performance of the company.

Fairness refers to protecting shareholders' rights and ensuring equitable treatment of all shareholders including minority and foreign shareholders, employees, communities and public officials (Ramaswamy, Ueng, & Carl, 2008). The *rationale* of the fairness principle in CG system is the following: the fairer the entity appears to stakeholders, the more likely it is that it can survive the pressure of interested parties. Therefore, 'the principle of fairness in corporate governance is not the form of fairness which ethics of justice is embedded in, namely the equitable allocation of resources and implementation of rules, but the equitable care distributed toward all stakeholders' (Tuan, 2012: 552). In addition, fairness can be disciplined differently, for instance, in the United Kngdom, fairness is regulated by the Companies Act 2006 (CA 06), while companies located in other countries prefer to have a shareholder agreement,[17] which can include more extensive and effective minority protection (Graves, 2005).

According to the last principle of CG, transparency, stakeholders ought to be informed in regard to the company's plans, activities and, above all, the risks involved in the implementations of the business strategies. More specifically, transparency involves a deep willingness by the company to clearly inform the stakeholders, for instance, about the performance reached by company truthfully and accurately so that all investors have access to clear, factual information which accurately reflects the financial, social and environmental position of the organisation. In addition, the roles and responsibilities of the board and management should be clarified and made publicly known to provide shareholders with a level of accountability. However, while scholars overall state that the most commonly discussed benefit of transparency is that it reduces asymmetric information, and hence lowers the cost of trading the firm's securities and the firm's cost of capital (Diamond & Verrecchia, 1991) other scholars argue that beyond a specific level of transparency profits start lowering (Hermalin, 2014).

Therefore, the main task of an efficient and effective CG system is that of adequately balancing all the principles described in order to allow the implementation of the creating value process. Overall, an efficient CG system depends on three main factors:

1 the quality of the laws that defines the structure, functioning and responsibilities of administrative and control bodies, supervisory authorities and jurisprudential bodies;
2 the ethical standards of those who actually have direct responsibilities in the functioning of the governance system;
3 stakeholders' education level.

We are all aware of the importance of good rules and the absence of holes in the regulatory system. However, there is an irreplaceable role played by ethical behaviour that should be able to guarantee a substantial compliance with the laws. However, responsible business behaviour is favoured by a social climate made up of strong expectations of good management and approval for those who seek to respond to these expectations. Good management has to be, firstly, recognised and surrounded by esteem, consent, gratitude. On the other hand, mismanagement must be disapproved and isolated in order to avoid the infection of the entire economic fabric.

Among the four principles described, the principle of accountability, so simple and even obvious, is actually the most frequently disregarded.

In fact, in companies firmly under the control of a controlling share-holder which, in fact, exercises the prerogatives of CG, most of the management responds directly to those who selected it and the boards of directors tend to function only in formal terms. In a public company, the principle of accountability is disregarded by who controls firmly the governance of the company by deciding the appointments of directors and auditors, selecting the information to be made available to the board of directors, making the board sign what is decided autonomously by the management, suppressing any criticism, even if it is constructive, in order to avoid conflicts. Therefore: *How is it possible to install the value of accountability in the behaviour of management, of the boards of directors, of the controlling shareholders?*

Different behaviours should be implemented in order to foster accountability, among others:

- all initiatives aimed, on the one hand, at affirming and disseminating, in the economic-social context and in the organisational context of the company, the culture of legality, of strict compliance with the rules; on the other hand, to counteract the culture of cunning, of merely formal compliance with the rules and their substantial avoidance;
- favouring everything that goes in the direction of introducing counterweights that serve to balance the power of the control groups and / or and/or CEOs, on the one hand, and the boards of directors on the other;
- implement internal control systems based on a supportive style, aimed at spreading a culture of self-control at all levels and in all organisational functions.

On the other hand, excessive sanctions, disproportionate to the seriousness of the violations, or punitive attitudes of errors in any case committed should be avoided as they feed the fear of giving bad news and candidly recognising management errors and inadequacies of the control system.

In order to measure the degree of efficiency and effectiveness of a CG system implemented and its ability to create value (performances) in a big corporation is a very arduous goal that is difficult to achieve in practice, since the process of creating value through is complex, characterised by the interaction of multiple variables and in fact it is impossible to measure the value created by every single variable. Theoretically, in order to be able to effectively carry out such a process of direct comparison, it would be necessary to compare at least two companies that are completely identical in terms of internal characteristics and environment in which they operate. However, those conditions of similarity are very unrealistic in practice.

Therefore, an indirect method to measure efficiency and effectiveness of CG seems to be more appropriate and realistic. The literature offers various possibilities to assess the degree of 'misalignment' between the value created for managers to the detriment of shareholders, which is actually the most important factor for those involved in CG assessment.

An interesting methodology, also for this analysis, is based on the so-called *Code of best practice* which will be explained in detail in chapter three.

Overall, a code of best practice is self-regulatory code in which recommendations are established, usually referring to companies whose shares are listed on a stock exchange, about the mechanisms and structures of CG that they represent. These codes do not usually have the force of law, but constitute a simple recommendation tool for companies, which are free to adapt, even partially, or not at all, to what is stated in them, with the sole constraint of having to indicate in the financial statement information their possible non-fulfilment. Obviously, pressure from investors will increasingly incentivize its application, avoiding investing in companies that do not comply with this legislation.

1.4 The Historical Evolution of Corporate Governance

Governing a company means making accurate choices regarding production strategies, financial and organisational structure, composition of fixed and variable capital, allocation of revenues, size and type of the investments and so on. It also means deciding which mergers and acquisitions are more appropriate in order to make the company grow, which activity sector to enter or exit for diversification or integration purposes or, on the other hand, if it is the case to dismiss any activity sector deemed unproductive. Last but not least, governing a company involves the decision on appointing or removing top managers. Based on this description, CG has always existed, only labelled it differently (Gallino, 2010).

However, CG studies are a relatively recent phenomenon, which experienced rapid development during the last decades of the twentieth century, even though entrepreneurs and company administrators have always paid great attention to the issue of CG. The design of governance structures and mechanisms took on relevance as such people began conducting their business through legal entities with legal personality and when firms became so large that their capital owners had to delegate the management to salaried managers.

The second industrial revolution imposed radical changes in the underlying structures of companies overwhelmed by the process of dimensional growth, especially companies operating in sectors characterised by a high intensity of capital and scientific research. Therefore, deep transformations in the ownership structures, financing systems and distribution of power within the company led to the beginning of the managerial enterprise (Marris, 1963), in which the ownership structures and the redistribution of authority within the company gravitate around owners, founders and families, who were required to assume new roles and attitudes towards the company.

Alfred Chandler (1977) describes the beginning of the managerial enterprises with the change of the role played by founding company members who began to look at the company from the point of view of pure rentiers just like the other shareholders. Therefore, their interest in the company was only related to the income they could gain from the company activities and no longer related to the management of the company which was delegated to salaried managers. In this new type of company, defined as managerial firm, representatives of the founding family do not intervene in the strategic decision making process.

Chandler's conclusions stem from research conducted in 1932 by a corporate lawyer, Adolf Berle, and an economist, Gardiner Means, who explained the foundations of managerial capitalism and the modern age of CG through the fact that managers started to have acquired more power than the owners. More specifically, Berle and Means examined the dispersion of ownership shares of the 200 America's largest non-financial corporations, concluding that in approximately 44% of the corporations, the operational control appeared to be transferred from ownership to salaried executives. In their opinion, the separation of ownership from control had occurred due to the fact that the ownership of the shares was dispersed among a large number of individuals and entities, of which none owned shares in sufficient quantity[18] to be able to concretely influence the management of the company. In addition, according to Berle and Means, the causes of the dispersion of the ownership had been mainly financial as the important technological changes that had occurred in the previous decades like the development of mass production techniques, which had given conspicuous advantages to already large companies to achieve economies of scale which, in turn, gave rise to gigantic industrial enterprises.

These large corporations required enormous volumes of capital, far in excess of the personal financial resources owned by any individual or rich families. Therefore, such businesses could only be financed by selling shares to many investors each of whom owned only a tiny fraction of the company's share capital with no possibility to either directly or indirectly intervene in the governance of the company. More specifically, company owners appeared to be confined to the passive role of rentiers of income in the form of profit while the role of the workers had been progressively diminishing in terms of relevance within the company.

In the 1950s and 1960s, the dominance of managerial capitalism, as exposed by Berle and Means, with its salaried managers dedicated to autonomously governing the company, more to the general interests of the company than to those of the owners, seemed an incontrovertible reality.

However, a large group of economists and sociologists supported the thesis that the separation between ownership and control described by Berle and Means was unfounded. This conclusion stemmed in part from the investigations of the Temporary National Economic Committee (Tnec), which pointed out that out of the 200 largest American corporations analysed by Berle and Means, 140 appeared to be controlled by large shareholders and, therefore, contrasting the conclusions reached by the authors.

This argument led to the conclusion according to which in the large corporations there is no justification for concluding that the management is separate from the ownership but, on the contrary, managers were and are among the major owners, due to the strategic positions they occupy and the role they play act as protectors and spokespersons of the whole property.

After this introduction, this chapter highlights the main points of the evolution of CG from the inception of the public company up to role of CG in the third millennium.

1.4.1 The Origin of the Public Company

At the beginning of the nineteenth century, entrepreneurs used to conduct their business through various alternative legal forms, none of which guaranteed the limited liability for the company's debts. In fact, in the case of insolvency of the company, creditors could claim back their credits on the assets of the shareholders and their families and this greatly limited the interest of investors in participating in companies.

During this period, the roles of investor and company director were both played by the entrepreneur. However, in the mid-nineteenth century, as the legal system allowed entrepreneurs to create a legal entity with its own rights, joint-stock company began to rise. This new type of company could take ownership of legal rights and responsibilities that were previously attributed only to natural persons who only bore the risk of temporarily owning the capital shares. Joint-stock companies also allowed the attribution to a specific set of rights to shareholders, including limited liability for the extent of the capital conferred, the right to vote in some important corporate decisions and the right to receive a portion of the residual return (profit) deriving from the exercise of business economic activity (dividend).

At the beginning of the twentieth century, some US and UK companies decided to list their shares on the capital market which led to two significant consequences: one, it significantly increased the number of shareholders and, two, it weakened their relationship with both the entrepreneur and the management team. The modern *public company*, characterised by the separation between shareholders (conferring risk capital) and managers (managing the company) through a widespread shareholding finally emerged and started to expand.

Therefore, the separation between ownership and control that occurs in public companies, where the person who manages the company or participates in the board of directors is a salaried manager who does not own shares in the company, gave rise to the debate on CG. In fact, the CG problem became evident because who manages the financial resources of others does not usually bare their task with the same vigilant attention that the owner would devote to it. In addition, the dilution of the shareholding structure among a large number of small investors allows managers of public companies to acquire control of the company and meet their personal interests at the expense of the shareholders.

During the years following the publication of the work of Berle and Means (1932), there are only a few notable contributions on the theme of CG. It was only during the 1960s that scholars began to address the topic more deeply.

1.4.1.1 The Sixties

During the 1960s, scholars began to address some questions and issues related to open corporation. More specifically, the separation between ownership and control that characterises American public companies led to the development of managerial theories.

These theories rejected the classic entrepreneurial model based on the owner-manager who manages the company with the aim of maximising profit by arguing that, at least in large companies with widespread shareholding, this objective was replaced with the pursuit of personal satisfaction of top corporate executives. However, managers' discretion was not unlimited, as they had to ensure a certain level of profit to implement an acceptable dividend policy, to finance the necessary investments for the development and protection of the solidity of the company, especially with credit institutions. In addition, managers' activities were always controlled even in the presence of a very fragmented shareholding structure.

In the sixties, an important mechanism implemented for the protection of shareholders' interests was represented by the markets (see paragraph 1.2.1). According to this mechanism, management must produce signals relating to its capabilities through the achievement of brilliant company results. Consequently, these positive signals would be necessary for the management as they allow it to create a good reputation on the job market over time and to exclude the possibility of being fired. On the other hand, unsatisfying business results, scandals or even the bankruptcy of the company would damage the reputation of the CEO and therefore severely compromising his/her hiring opportunities. Based on the abovementioned considerations, the management is therefore pushed to manage their relationship with the company wisely by engaging and supervising employees.

Reputation would then solve all agency problems established between management and shareholders, allowing management to have greater expectations in the job market and to obtain salary increases from the company. On the other hand, bad management will suffer, in addition to the consequences explained above, also strong from competition from candidates holding lower positions in the corporate hierarchy. From the negative consequences mentioned, managers are therefore expected to be motivated in order to implement a policy of increasing corporate value.

Overall, the fundamental requirement for the efficient functioning of the market is its ability to correctly evaluate the value of a company's shares. In the presence of an efficient capital market, the market price of a company's shares fully reflects the quality of management decisions and consequently, the share value of a company which, if not properly managed, will fall to a value low enough to incentivize some investors to acquire its control.

1.4.1.2 The Seventies

In the seventies, the attention of scholars and public opinion is focused on three main themes:

1   in both the United States and the Great Britain, the results of academic research and the bankruptcy of some large corporations pushed the supervisory bodies on the stock exchange and listed companies to request greater independence of directors and to encourage the introduction of control committees;
2   in Europe, the harmonisation process of the company law at the European level was at the centre of the attention of exponents of both the industrial and political scene;
3   there was traction of the school of thought aimed at expanding the social responsibilities of companies and affirming a broader notion of stakeholders that, in addition to shareholders, included employees, suppliers, customers, lenders, the government and the community in the broad sense.

Regarding the first point, in the United States, the debate started with the publication of an empirical research concerning the composition and functioning of the boards of directors within large companies. The study showed that companies used to evaluate their directors based on their personal charisma and not on the contribution they could make to the functioning of the board. Therefore, the board of directors was not able to effectively carry out most of the tasks assigned and, therefore, unable to contribute to the achievement of the medium/long-term corporate results. Consequently, the bankruptcy of many large listed companies fuelled the debate on the functioning of the board of directors and led some dissatisfied investors to withdraw their investments by asking the directors of these companies for the reimbursement of the capital invested in their company. In order to decrease the number of bankruptcies, numerous proposals were made. One of them required the increase in the number of independent external directors[19] and the introduction of audit committees which had already been recommended in the late 1930s by the New York Stock Exchange (NYSE) and the Securities and Exchange Commission (SEC).

Regarding the second point, one of the elements that boosted the debate on CG during the 1970s concerned the harmonisation process of the company law among the member states of the European Economic Community (EEC). More specifically, one of the proposals that led to great tensions among the representatives of various countries was the fifth, drawn up in 1972. This directive proposal recommended companies operating in the member states of the European Community abandon the *one-tier* CG system[20], based on the board of directors at one level, and replace it with the *two-tier* CG system implemented by German and Dutch corporations. More specifically, within the two-tier system, there is an executive board that has the task of managing the company and a supervisory board, which is responsible for appointing the members of the executive board and supervising their work. However, this proposal did not complete its procedural process due to the aversion of some Member States towards the introduction of a two-level board of directors, but also due to the hypothesis of co-determination[21] which gives economic power to those who control the means of production and uses employee participation as a tool to counter the interests of capital (Pistor, 1999: 163).

In regard to the third point, the debate mainly concerned the role played by large multinationals. In particular, at the beginning of the seventies, a school of thought emerged by confronting the liberal principle according to which companies must create value for shareholders and, in doing so, companies contribute to the economic and social development of the community. According to those who contested this principle, the orientation towards maximising profit and creating economic value for shareholders had some negative consequences for the community such as environmental pollution, the exploitation of child labour, poor health conditions for both employees and the community in general. Therefore, protesters believed that companies should not have had to limit themselves to creating value for shareholders only, but they should have had to meet the expectations of all company's stakeholders such as employees, consumers, suppliers, lenders, government and the local community. Therefore, as the size of large corporations is restlessly increasing, its impact under social and environmental point of view could no longer be neglected.

1.4.1.3 The Eighties

In the early 1980s, the debate on CG seemed to slowly decrease, especially in the United States and Great Britain, where the Reagan and Thatcher governments were pursuing policies, based on economic liberalism, which aimed at strengthening the responsibility of directors towards shareholders and reaffirming the principle of profit maximisation as a guiding criterion for companies. However, some negative events that occurred at the end of the eighties reawakened the interest of both public opinion and industrial world in CG issues. More specifically, some big corporations and investment banks were overwhelmed by financial scandals triggered by the use of illegal practices of some entrepreneurs and board members. These negative events reawakened the debate on the composition and functioning of the boards of directors. In particular, on the one side, they highlighted the excessive influence of top management and the CEO on the decisions taken by the board of directors and, on the other side, they reaffirmed the need to create counterweight mechanisms of control aimed at giving greater power to non-executive directors.

The loss of competitiveness occurred towards the end of the 1980s to the American economic system in comparison with the German and Japanese systems represented a further reason for increasing the interest in CG issues. In particular, the loss of competitiveness was mainly due to high cost of capital; lack of effectiveness of the internal control systems; excessive emphasis of reward systems that link the remuneration of managers to company performance in the short-term press and high pressure exerted by financial market towards the publication of brilliant company results every quarter.

An additional element that drew the attention of both public opinion and academics to CG issues was the high number of hostile takeovers,[22] leveraged buyouts (LBOs)[23] and corporate restructurings.[24] These activities occurred in the second half of the 1980s in the United States and United Kingdom and resulted in high financial debt and strong concentration of capital with a few key shareholders.

A further phenomenon that occurred during the 1980s boosted the interest of scholars and public opinion in CG was an enormous increase in terms of remuneration of the CEOs paid by Anglo-Saxon corporations. More specifically, the debate concerned two fundamental aspects: CEOs received salaries only comparable with that of the stars of the entertainment and sports world; the salary was weakly linked with company performance. However, the defenders of the *status quo* of CEO rejected these accusations and argued that the compensation received by the top manager is linked to the performance of the company in the medium and long term, while in the short time, company's results could even be negative and it was not due to CEOs' negative performance.

Finally, in the 1980s, there was the beginning of the downsizing process which involved a very high number of large companies. This phenomenon arose as a reaction to the loss of competitiveness that characterised the US industrial system in the 1980s. The consequent wave of layoffs involved, firstly, only small and medium-sized corporations but, eventually, it spread to large corporations such as Exxon, General Electric, IBM, General Motors and Procter and Gamble, all companies where employees were guaranteed safe and well-paid jobs. Consequently, top managers were soon fired by shareholders who were not satisfied with their performance.

1.4.1.4 The Nineties

During the nineties, the concept of CG crossed the boundaries of scholars and businessmen and drew the attention of politicians and public opinion due to few events that occurred during this period:

1   the fall of the Soviet socialist regime;
2   the privatisation of entire economic sectors in different nations;
3   the growing weight of institutional investors in the risk capital of large companies;
4   the sudden bankruptcy of some leading industrial and financial companies;
5   the progressive integration of international financial markets and
6   the carrying out of some large acquisitions.

A first event that drew attention to the issue of CG was the sudden political and economic collapse of the Soviet Union. This event established the superiority of economic systems based on free individual entrepreneurial initiatives and opened the discussion regarding the best way to manage the transition from a centrally planned economy to an economy based on the free market. More specifically, the efficient functioning of a market economy required, in fact, the introduction of important changes in the governance and management systems of companies, in the economic and legal infrastructures that were necessary to encourage and protect free entrepreneurial initiatives and, finally, in the values and knowledge of the people operating within the economic system.

The second event that assumed relevance during the nineties is represented by the massive process of privatisation and liberalisation of entire sectors of the national economy undertaken by some countries of the industrialised world while the UK and the US governments had undertaken a liberal economic policy the previous decade.

The third event that occurred in the 1990s, closely related to the privatisation process, was the growing role played by institutional investors in the share capital of large listed companies. More specifically, the restless growth of portfolios managed by institutional investors forced them to acquire large shares of the main companies listed on various stock markets and this enabled them to exert a great influence on the decisions taken by the governing bodies of the investee companies. Therefore, while previously institutional investors, by holding only modest quantities of shares in listed companies, could freely move their investment portfolios through the acquisition of securities issued by efficiently managed companies and selling those of companies that did not perform well on the market, the increase in the share capital held in each company made the exit option no longer easily feasible. As a result of these dynamics, mutual fund managers were forced to change their strategy, from an exit strategy to a strategy based on the creation of communication channels and participation in shareholders' meetings and, therefore, influence the company's decisions on different matters such as the composition of the board of directors, the remuneration of the directors, the transparency of information provided, etc.

The fourth event involved the bankruptcy of some important companies and the discovery of serious corporate crimes committed by the top management of these companies, fuelling the debate in the United Kingdom on how companies were governed. The reaction of the country's financial and industrial community led to the establishment of a committee, chaired by Adrian Cadbury, which was entrusted with the task of drafting a report on the CG of large British companies. The report and the code of best practices annexed to it largely emphasises the role of independent external directors and the audit committee in balancing and controlling the steering power of executive directors. The code was not mandatory for listed companies, however, the market started to morally persuade companies of the needed improvement of their CG practices. The publication of the Cadbury report represented an important moment in the debate on CG at a national and global level. In fact, numerous industrialised countries followed the British experience by supporting the creation of committees, composed of authoritative exponents in the industrial and financial world, which were charged with drawing up codes of conduct on CG issues.

The fifth event that occurred in the 1990s, which fuelled the debate on CG during the 1990s, is represented by the progressive integration of international financial markets into a single global market. This phenomenon was the result of dynamics that affect both the demand side and the supply side of financial resources. More specifically, in regard to the demand side, big corporations in every country constantly looked for sources of financing that could guarantee the necessary resources to fuel the growth process. On the supply side, institutional investors, especially those of Anglo-Saxon origin, were continuously looking for new markets to invest in the growing amount of financial resources raised by savers. However, the convergence of national capital markets into a single global market presented not only benefits but some risks as well like the financial crisis that initially hit some emerging countries in the Eastern Europe and the Far East or South America and then it spread rapidly throughout the world economic system. Subsequently, the representatives of some important international organisations such as the International Monetary Fund, the World Bank, the Organisation for Development and Economic Cooperation (OECD) and the United Nations that the solution to the deep financial crisis occurred was not linked only to macroeconomic interventions but it had to pass through a reform of CG aimed at guaranteeing greater protection of minority shareholders.

Finally, the last event occurred in the nineties involved the great wave of mergers and acquisitions that had characterised American and British corporations in the eighties and then it involved many European companies. The acquisitions made in this period involved both companies located in the same country and companies that have their legal headquarters in different countries (cross border). Among the most important operation carried out at the European level, there was the hostile acquisition of the German *Mannesmann* by the *British Vodafone*, for an amount exceeding 190 billion dollars, while in Italy, *Telecom Italia* was acquired by Olivetti for an amount exceeding 60 billion euros.[25]

These operations introduced in Europe an instrument, typical of Anglo-Saxon capitalist systems. In this situation, even more surprising was the attitude of the public authorities who maintained a certain detachment and did not oppose the passage of control of important national companies into the hands of foreign competitors.

1.4.2 *Corporate Governance in the New Millennium*

Even at the beginning of twenty-first century, the debate on CG was fuelled by the occurrence of some episodes that led academics and representatives of the political and economic world to question themselves about the existence of the best model of CG suitable for manufacturing companies and financial intermediaries. In particular, these episodes explained the rise and decline of the value of *new economy*[26] securities and the umpteenth wave of corporate scandals that involved some large companies in numerous industrialised countries (Black & Lynch, 2004).

The first event that emotionally and above all economically affected savers is represented by the speculative bubble also known as *dot.com bubble* (Goodnight & Green, 2010), caused by the excessive speculation of Internet-related companies between 1995 and March 2000 when the Nasdaq Composite stock market index rose 400% and, then rapidly fell 78% from its peak in few months. The rapid growth of the Internet generated frenetic confusion among investors, who quickly invested their financial resources into start-up companies that can raise enough money to go public lacking, however, of a business plan, product, or track record of profits. Consequently, many online shopping and communications companies such as *Pets.com, Waban, Boo.com, WorldCom, North Point,* and *Global Crossing* had to shut down and savers ended up losing all their money.

However, the speculative bubble cannot be attributed exclusively to the excessive optimism of numerous entrepreneurs and venture capitalists towards the potential inherent in new technologies related to the Internet, but requires careful investigation of the behaviour of numerous individuals who have drawn huge gains from the rise in the share price of the Internet-related companies, in particular:

- shareholders of the company who fuelled the share prices in order to make large capital gains;
- financial intermediaries such as venture capital firms, banks, mutual funds and insurance companies that, in order to receive large placement commissions, placed company shares on the market at very high values, despite their uncertain value;
- information intermediaries such as auditors, financial analysts, bond-rating agencies, and the financial press that continued to attribute constantly rising target prices to the shares of companies that often did not have a net profit or even had a negative operating profit.

The second event is represented by the financial scandals that evidently show how the control system in place was not able to highlight in time the illegal practices undertaken by the top management and directors of these companies who were accused of several crimes such as financial fraudulent reporting (Beasley, Carcello, & Hermanson, 2000), misappropriation of assets (Coram, Ferguson, & Moroney, 2008), corruption and insider trading[27] (King & Roell, 1988).

These negative episodes have struck public opinion as they involved many leading companies considered excellent even by the same auditing firms that certify their financial statements, therefore, causing considerable damage to many categories of stakeholders such as shareholders, bondholders and employees. In order to avoid a drastic reduction in the financial resources invested, the national and international authorities introduced new rules[28] aimed at attributing higher civil and criminal liabilities to people who commit corporate crimes with the aim of protecting the interest of those whose finance businesses without being able to influence the management's behaviour. Based upon what has been mentioned so far, we can firmly assert that the most serious consequence of the reckless behaviour adopted by the management is not so much the patrimonial damage swiftly inflicted on savers who had purchased bonds and shares of companies that went bankrupt but 'the loss of community and savers' trust' towards the industrial and financial world and all the subjects and authorities responsible for supervising the accuracy of the corporate behaviour.

1.5 Corporate Social Responsibility (CSR)

The corporate scandals occurred in the 1990s and at the beginning of the third millennium as a result of the legally correct but reckless management strategies led to a huge capital loss and, above all, the loss of savers' faith in the economic and industrial system. Consequently, the inadequate CG practices of some large companies, in which many citizens have invested their savings, have driven public attention to the integrity and attitude of companies towards shareholders and society as a whole.

We may define irresponsible a company that, beyond its legal obligations, assumes that it does not have to answer to any public and private authority, or public opinion, regarding the economic, social and environmental consequences of its activities. Among these activities should be mentioned: the industrial and financial strategies implemented; the working conditions offered to employees in the country and abroad; the impact of products and production processes on the environment; the usage of financial funds that have been entrusted to it by savers in the form of shares or bonds; the drafting of financial statements; the quality of the manufactured products; the type and quality of the relationships established with the communities in which the company operates; the locations or relocations are chosen to carry out the production activities and the compliance with tax regulations.

The spread of irresponsible enterprise is the consequence of two main causes. Firstly, the development of a new business concept based on the maximisation of its market value on the stock exchange at any cost, regardless of its turnover or production size. Theoretically, this new business concept would seem to favour anyone who owns even a single share, were it not for its practical applications during the 1990s and early 2000s when only the owners of large quantity of shares and the managers who implemented their directives got enormous profits from it, while holders of a few corporate stocks or bonds saw quick evaporation of their value and therefore ending up losing all their savings. Secondly, the modification of the structure and functioning of the CG bodies in order to affirm, in practice, the conception of the shareholders' value, and this gave the power back to the owners, of a traditional type (family capitalism), but also of new type represented by institutional investors such as private and public pension funds, investment funds and insurance companies. Consequently, the irresponsible management led to corporate scandals that exploded initially in the United States and then spread to all Europe.

Among the socially irresponsible actions, it is worth mentioning:

• indecent wages and working conditions for hundreds of thousands of employees, sometimes even minors;
• the construction in developing countries of unsafe chemical plants that killed thousands of innocent people (India 1984);
• employment of slave workers (Ivory Coast 2002); tens of thousands of children who work in inhuman conditions, due to the harmfulness of the chemicals used, in Indian farms that grow cotton then supplied to multinationals (India 2004);
• the sudden dismissal of thousands of employees via SMS and voicemail;
• release of pollution into the air, water and workplaces caused by the large public and private chemical industry for decades with thousands of cases of cancer linked to the processing of asbestos.
• the partial or total closure, or the actual or threatened relocation in order to have greater flexibility in exchange carried out by multinational groups that justify their irresponsible behaviour with lousy reasons such as that other units in the group achieve higher profits; due to the merger with another group, some plant or department has become a superfluous duplicate; the shutdown of some units is necessary within the framework of an overall rationalisation of the group's productions. Such interventions result in the loss of hundreds of jobs in local communities where such businesses were a major source of employment and income.

The core of the argument is that irresponsible business is not only the matter of people, more specifically, of managers more or less inclined to commit white-collar crimes. However, irresponsible business is the result of a structural model which specifically aims at increasing market value of the company. Consequently, owners either incentivize or oblige managers to pursue shareholder value creation by precisely complying with the guidelines provided. On the other hand, the media hardly ever discuss how and by whom the companies are really governed. In addition, the degree of responsibility does not depend on the size of a company. In fact, there are small and medium companies in a more irresponsible way than large companies. However, in the case of a large company or of a group of companies controlled by a financial company, with thousands of employees, the effects of the actions that it may carry out irresponsibly affect a much greater number of people than in small companies. After this brief overview, we can say that the inadequate CG practices of some large companies, in which many citizens have invested their savings, have drawn public attention to the integrity and attitude of companies towards shareholders and society as a whole. Nowadays, companies are required to account for their impact on society, therefore, taking social responsibility for their actions.

Both at national and international level, the need to control the impacts of the organisations management activities on stakeholders has emerged to pursue the ultimate goal of an integrated and balanced approach among economic, social and environmental factors and performance shared with stakeholders. This approach is called *corporate social responsibility (CSR)* and companies have started allocating resources to the implementation of socially responsible activities.

CSR refers to 'a set of ideas and perspectives about business practice that its advocates anticipate to see widely implemented through the corporate sector' (Gainer, 2010; Tuan, 2012: 547). Du, Bhattacharya and Sen (2010) state that, through CSR activities, companies can simultaneously reinforce both stakeholder–company bondings and corporate image.

By adopting CSR practices, organisations can guarantee a holistic approach to the management of business risks, aiming at satisfying the needs of all the stakeholders involved: this allows to balance the interests of the company, of the capital market, of the shareholders, of the control bodies, employees, customers, suppliers and the company as a whole, providing them with the utmost transparency in management and demonstrating consistency with declared and expected values, principles and behaviours and with the ultimate goal of long-term value creation. Scholars have highlighted an increasing interaction and impact between CSR and CG (Gill, 2008; Charbaji, 2009). More specifically, a strong

CG lays the foundations for a good CSR through value-creating relationship with all stakeholders (Shahin & Zairi, 2007; Welford, 2007).

Even though profit is still a binding reference for businesses today, something is changing, albeit slowly. In fact, the attention begins to focus on how to produce profit and no longer only on 'how much' profit an organisation can produce. On the other hand, Henderson (2005) includes profit making in the company's social responsibilities. In this regard, Carroll (1991) places CSR at the bottom of the hierarchy of firm's responsibilities while economic and legal responsibilities at the top of the hierarchy. Within the CSR approach, stakeholders play a central role, in fact, Hopkins (2012) defines CSR as being concerned with stakeholders treated responsibly[29] and ethically by the firm that has both economic and environmental responsibilities. Therefore, socially responsible organisations has to create higher standards of living for their stakeholders while conserving organisation profitability.

Overall, an organisation can create value when its management pursues the goal of sustainability. A sustainable corporation aims at developing and reconciling economic, social and environmental dimensions, and it is considered as a socially and ethically responsible company able to increase its own intangible assets of knowledge and trust. Moreover, sustainability requires the usage of new systems of evaluation and reporting correct in order to provide an in-depth examination of company performance which can no longer be only at economic but also at social and environmental levels through the usage of different social and environmental sustainability assessment methodologies developed throughout the years.

1.5.1 Verification Tools and Social Reporting Models

The attention voluntarily given by companies to environmental, ethical and social aspects involves the following: one, the need to externally communicate their non-economic performance achieved, and two, there is a rising interest of the community in data that can be verified by an external body. More specifically, the external body, due to its quality of *super partes* third party, can issue a certification guaranteeing the accuracy of what is stated by the company. This avoids the danger for the company of being self-referential and allows citizens to verify that the social commitment advertised by the company is actually implemented and maintained over time. Different tools and models for reporting on social and environmental companies' performance have been developed over the years to clearly distinguish companies that, with their initiatives, have obtained results to meet the requirements requested by the certification body.

The need increasingly felt by modern industry to communicate its social responsibility and present itself to the public with a recognisable label has however led to the proliferation of different standards at national and international levels. The great variety of standards available has the undesirable side effect of increasing uncertainty around the concept of CSR for both companies and stakeholders. In fact, it is hard to recognise whether the certification, label or management system can guarantee higher compatibility with the ethical and sustainable values pursued. Any tool or social reporting model can be more correctly assessed by taking the perspective of the stakeholders to which it refers and considering the real impact that the initiatives taken by the company and specified in the model have on them.

1.5.1.1 Social Accountability 8000

Social Accountability 8000 (SA 8000) is an auditable certification standard that aims at inspiring organisations to develop, preserve and implement socially acceptable practices within the workplace. The SA 8000 Standard and Certification System provide a framework for organisations of all types, in any industry, and in any country to fairly and civilly run their business especially in regard to employees and, above all, to show their compliance with the highest social standards. The main principle of SA 8000 is that better working conditions will undoubtedly benefit the whole company as well as in terms of productivity, stakeholder relationships, market access, etc.

SA 8000 was created by the Social Accountability International in 1997, and it has a leading role since then. As of June 2021, there are 4668 certified organisations employing 2,180,617 people and operating in 56 industries in 58 different countries.[30] However, only SA 8000 certificates issued by audit firms validated by Social Accountability Accreditation Services can be accepted by stakeholders as a true indicator of social performance.

In practice, a company can assess its social performance if it can demonstrate its compliance with eight social performance criteria:

1   No use or support of child labour under any circumstances;
2   No use or support for forced labour under any circumstances;
3   Obligation to provide a safe and health workplace;
4   Obligation to respect the right to both form and join trade unions;

5   No use or support of discrimination based on race, national or social origin, caste, birth, religion, disability, gender, sexual orientation, union membership, political opinions and age under any circumstances;

6   Obligation to treat employees respectfully;

7   Obligation to strictly follow laws and industry standards regarding working hours;

8   Respect right of personnel of living salary.

These criteria should be considered as the minimum requirements rather than a guarantee of high quality. The SA 8000 certification system guarantees the ethicality of the production processes of specific goods or services on the market, and it also promotes the external diffusion of ethical and moral values shared by the certified company.

1.5.1.2 Global Reporting Initiative (GRI)

The GRI is an international independent institution that aims at helping organisations communicate their economic, social and environmental impact in a comparable and unique manner. More specifically, in order to respond to the increasing pressure exerted on different types of stakeholders such as governments, consumers and investors about being transparent, companies nowadays have to issue a sustainability report. GRI produces the world's most broadly used standards for sustainability reporting, the so-called GRI Standards. GRI model is based on the assumption according to which reporting is a clear sign of taking responsibility, and responsible organisations have to be straightforward and open with their stakeholders. On the other hand, organisations can better comprehend and manage their impact on people and the environment through clear reporting.

GRI is not so much a performance standard but rather a measurement system aimed at helping organisations draw up a report that includes indicators of social, environmental and economic nature. The GRI standards and guidelines are issued to help organisations draft the sustainability report aim at favouring sustainable development, in a perspective in which environmental factors appear privileged over the others. Hence it represents, like other models, a system that alone does not guarantee compliance with all the variables necessary to measure the degree of integration and implementation of the CSR.

GRI was founded in 1997 by the US-based non-profits *Coalition for Environmentally Responsible Economies (Ceres)* and *Tellus Institute* with the support of the *United Nations Environment Programme*

(UNEP). GRI issued the first 'exposure draft' version of the Sustainability Reporting Guidelines in 1999 and the first full version in 2000. Nowadays, the majority of multinational organisations, governments, small and medium enterprises (SMEs), non-governmental organizations (NGOs) and industry groups in more than 90 countries are currently using the GRI's sustainability reporting standards, which continue to be updated and added to, including new Topic Standards on Tax (2019) and Waste (2020).[31] Today, the GRI's headquarter is located in Amsterdam with a network of seven regional hubs, more specifically in Johannesburg (Africa), Singapore (ASEAN), São Paulo (Brazil), Hong Kong (Greater China Region), Bogota (Hispanic America), New York (North America) and New Delhi (South Asia).

1.5.1.3 Eco-Management and Audit Scheme (EMAS)

At European level, the European Commission introduced the Eco-Management and Audit Scheme (EMAS) as a not mandatory management instrument for private or public organisations operating inside or outside the European borders, willing to evaluate, report and improve their environmental performance.

The EMAS regulation represents the most evident expression of the new approaches to the environmental protection policy of the European Union in order to make the principle of sustainability effective and, above all, voluntarily. EMAS, in fact, encourages the voluntary adhesion of any type of organisation to environmental registration and certification in order to increase their competition activity and efficiency, thus reducing the impacts and waste generated.

The key principles to which the organisations must be inspired by in pursuing the eco-management path are:

1   performance: organisations have to improve their environmental performance by assessing and decreasing their environmental impact;
2   credibility: the external and independent EMAS registration process is guaranteed by a third-party verification;
3   transparency: organisations have to provide public information on their environmental performance both internally through the involvement of employees and externally through the issue of environmental statements.

In order to obtain an EMAS's certification, an organisation have to complete few main steps[32]:

- contacting the competent body;
- conducting an initial environment review;
- structuring the Environmental Management System (EMS) by defining an environmental policy and an environmental program;
- implementing the EMS;
- assessing the effectiveness of the EMS through an internal environmental audit;
- aiming to restlessly increase your environmental performance;
- drafting the environmental report;
- obtaining the verification of the EMS and the validation of the environmental report;
- sending the EMS and report to the European EMAS register;
- promoting the EMAS logo to show the company's environmental commitment to customers, suppliers and authorities.

In order to promote the best practices, EMAS presents the EMAS Awards for company that have demonstrated clear environment excellence in one of the six categories: private micro and small organisations; private medium-sized organisations; private large organisations; public micro and small organisations and public medium-sized and large organisations. Last EMAS Awards was held in Spain in 2019.

1.5.1.4 Social Reporting Tools

Undertaking CSR policies and actions is a voluntary choice made by the organisation's management, which decides how to act towards various stakeholders and society as a whole. CSR implies the usage of tools aimed at its implementation and subsequent reporting.

Among the main social reporting tools, there are:

- Environmental balance: it is a tool that reports on the environmental policies implemented across the board by the administration through physical indicators connected to policies and it also reports the destination of the expenditure incurred for environmental purposes.
- Social report: it is one of the most used tools for social reporting, which is an autonomous document separate from the accounting documents through which the company reports its social performance through a series of qualitative and quantitative indicators. This type of document is complementary to the financial statements, and often, for accuracy, tends to clarify the content of some of its items.

- Sustainability report: the natural evolution of the Social Report and the Environmental Balance is represented by the Sustainability Report, which aims at accounting for the impacts generated with respect to both environmental and social dimension. The sustainability report is intended to be a complete and easy-to-read document that allows the stakeholder to quickly obtain the information they need to evaluate the company as a whole.
- Integrated report: it represents the latest evolution of the sustainability management process in a company. This document goes beyond sustainability, and it expands the economic reporting addressed to shareholders and the financial community according to the 'Triple Bottom Line' approach: economic sustainability, social sustainability and environmental sustainability (Slaper & Hall, 2011).

1.5.1.5 Social Return on Investment (SROI)

Different organisations and academic institutions have been developing a great variety of social impact evaluation methods throughout the years. Among them, we have Social Enterprise Balanced Scorecard (BSC); third sector performance dashboard; Ongoing assessment of social impact (OASIS); Social Return Assessment (SRA); Social Accounting and Auditing (SAA); Social Impact Measurement for Local Economies (SIMPLE); Benefit–Cost ratio; SROI; Social e-valuator; Basic Efficiency Resource analysis (BER); Best Available Charitable Option Ratio (BACO); Cost per impact and Expected Return.

Among them, SROI represents one of the most established social impact assessment methods (Lombardo, Mazzocchetti, Rapallo, Tayser, & Cincotti, 2019: 2). More specifically, SROI is an approach utilised to evaluate the value created by organisations operating in private, public and non-profit sector. This tool was first developed and promoted in the non-profit sector by the Roberts Economic Development Fund (REDF) in 1996. Since then, its usage has been broadly extended both at the academic and operational levels. The rationale behind REDF's willingness to assess their resources' impact was that of evaluating how much people's lives were actually improving (Gair, 2002) and, at the same time, broadening the traditional concept of financial return by enclosing 'who' the return was linked to and including all the elements contributing to the production of the return.

Since its first application, SROI has been gradually modified, and integrated with principles and processes usually applied to economic and financial assessment (e.g. return on investment - ROI). It aimed at assessing an intervention under social, economic and environmental points of view, known as the triple bottom line (Norman & MacDonald, 2004), due to the fact that each investment has to yield social, economic and environmental returns to create blended value (Emerson, 2003).

Organisations willing to calculate the SROI have to take six main steps:[33]

1   Establishing scope and identifying key stakeholders;
2   Mapping outcomes.
3   Evidencing outcomes and giving them a value.
4   Establishing impact.
5   Calculating the SROI.
6   Reporting, using and embedding.

Even though SROI calculation has been exponentially increasing in the past twenty years, there are few obstacles to its complete reliability in both the academic and business world. Among them, there is the fact that some benefits cannot be expressed in monetary terms which seems to be the main focus in the SROI calculation. SROI is a time and resource-consuming, therefore, some organisations cannot afford to calculate the social impact of their activities. Lastly, results have to be properly interpreted in order to avoid inaccurate attributions of merit to underserving stakeholders.

Notes

1 The word corporate stems from the word *corporation* which refers to American term used to define a large public company. The word *Governance* comes from the Latin word *gubernare* and it means *driving*.
2 Cicero, *De Senectute.*
3 It is the British self-regulatory code drawn up in 1992 by the commission set up in May 1991 and chaired by Sir. Adrian Cadbury due to serious financial scandals that occurred at that time. The commission was based on the initiative of the London Stock Exchange, the Financial Reporting Council, the Confederation of British Industry and the Accountancy Profession.
4 Committee on the Financial Aspects of Corporate Governance. (1992). *Report with code of best practice* [Cadbury Report]. London: Gee Publishing.
5 Privatisation is an operation by which a significant (or totalitarian) part of the ownership of a public company passes into the hands of private shareholders through the purchase of the organisation shares.

6 *Le nuove funzioni degli organi societari: verso la corporate governance?*
(2002). Convegno Courmayeur, Giuffrè.
7 https://www.sebi.gov.in/reports/reports/mar-2003/the-report-of-shri-n-r-narayana-murthy-committee-on-corporate-governance-for-public-comments-_12986.html
8 Fiori, G. (2003). *Corporate governance e qualità dell'informazione esterna di impresa.* Milano: Giuffrè.
9 Residual right stems from the fact that shareholders have a residual claim on a company's assets because creditors, debtors and other preferential shareholders are usually paid first.
10 A complete contract aims at eliminating all possible opportunistic behaviours by perfectly defining each contracting party rights and responsibilities with no discretion gap left.
11 Data and results manipulations led in many cases to big scandals (see page 4).
12 Insider trading is the trading of a public company's stock or other securities (such as bonds or stock options) based on the disclosure of non-public information about the company.
13 Members of the board of directors could represent different interest groups such as banks and employees.
14 For instance, Enron, WorldCom and Parmalat.
15 According to Grossman and Hart, 5% of the shares qualifies a shareholder as Blockholder.
16 https://www.icaew.com/-/media/corporate/files/library/subjects/corporate-governance/financial-aspects-of-corporate-governance.ashx?la=en
17 A shareholders' agreement is a settlement among the shareholders in a company to regulate the relationship between the shareholders, the management of the company, ownership of the shares and the protection of the shareholders.
18 Each of the fifteen or twenty largest shareholders of each corporation own less than 3% of the ownership shares.
19 Directors who have no economic relationship with the company.
20 Directors have the same responsibilities.
21 Codetermination is a practice where workers of an enterprise have the right to vote for representatives on the board of directors in a company.
22 The target company is bought by another company, called the acquirer, by going directly to the company's shareholders or fighting to replace management to get the acquisition approved.
23 A company acquires another company using a significant amount of borrowed money to meet the cost of acquisition. The assets of the company being acquired are often used as collateral for the loans, along with the assets of the acquiring company.
24 The acquisition of control of the company and the subsequent restructuring activity make it possible to increase corporate efficiency through the reduction of overheads and the sale of business units not strictly connected to the core business.
25 https://www.nytimes.com/1999/05/22/business/olivetti-prevails-in-hostile-bid-for-far-bigger-telecom-italia.html
26 This New Economy is characterised by companies increasing their capital investments in information-technology software and hardware.

27 The exploitation of information not in the public domain, the disclosure of which will have effects in the quotations of securities, for transactions carried out on the stock exchange taking advantage of their advance knowledge.
28 For instance, the Public Company Accounting Reform and Investor Protection Act issued in the USA in 2002.
29 Ethically or responsibly means treated in a manner deemed acceptable in civilised society.
30 http://www.saasaccreditation.org/?q=node/23
31 https://www.globalreporting.org/about-gri/mission-history/
32 https://ec.europa.eu/environment/emas/join_emas/how_does_it_work_step0_en.htm
33 https://www.thinknpc.org/wp-content/uploads/2018/07/SROI-position-paper.pdf

References

Amihud, Y., & Stoyanov, S. (2017). Do staggered boards harm shareholders?. *Journal of Financial Economics*, *123*(2), 432–439. doi: 10.1016/j.jfineco.2016.04.002.

Beasley, M. S., Carcello, J. V., Hermanson, D. R., & Lapides, P. D. (2000). Fraudulent financial reporting: Consideration of industry traits and corporate governance mechanisms. *Accounting Horizons*, *14*(4), 441–454.

Berle Adolf A., & Means Gardiner, C. (1932). *The modern corporation and private property*. New York: Macmillan.

Besanko, D., Dranove, D., Shanley, M., & Schaefer, S. (2004). The vertical boundaries of the firm. *Economics of Strategy, Kapitel*, *3*(3), 105–139.

Black, S. E., & Lynch, L. M. (2004). What's driving the new economy?: The benefits of workplace innovation. *The Economic Journal*, *114*(493), F97–F116. doi: 10.1111/j.0013-0133.2004.00189.x

Cadbury, A. (2002). *Corporate governance and chairmanship: A personal view*. Oxford University Press on Demand.

Carroll, A.B. (1991). The pyramid of corporate social responsibility: toward the moral management of organizational stakeholders, *Business Horizons*, July/August, 39–48.

Chandler, Alfred D., Jr. (1977). *The visible hand: The managerial revolution in American business*. Cambridge, MA: Harvard University Press.

Charbaji, A. (2009). The effect of globalization on commitment to ethical corporate governance and corporate social responsibility in Lebanon. *Social Responsibility Journal*, 5(3), 376–387. doi:10.1108/17471110910977294

Chen, L. J., & Chen, S. Y. (2011). How the pecking-order theory explain capital structure. *Journal of International Management Studies*, *6*(3), 92–100.

Coase, R. H. (1937). The nature of the firm. *Economica*, New Series, *4*(16), 386–405.

Colli, A. (2006). *Corporate Governance e assetti proprietari. Dinamiche e comparazioni internazionali*. Venezia: Marsilio.

Coram, P., Ferguson, C., & Moroney, R. (2008). Internal audit, alternative internal audit structures and the level of misappropriation of assets fraud. *Accounting & Finance, 48*(4), 543–559. doi:10.1111/j.1467-629x.2007.00247.x

Dcmsetz, H. (1983). The structure of ownership and the theory of the firm. *The Journal of Law and Economics, 26*(2), 375–390.

DePamphilis, D. (2010). *Mergers and acquisitions basics: All you need to know.* Burlington, USA: Academic Press.

Diamond, D. W., & Verrecchia, R. E. (1991). Disclosure, liquidity, and the cost of capital. *The journal of Finance, 46*(4), 1325–1359.

Du, S., Bhattacharya, C. B., & Sen, S. (2010). Maximizing business returns to corporate social responsibility (CSR): The role of CSR communication. *International Journal of Management Reviews, 12*(1), 8–19.

Emerson, J. (2003). The blended value proposition: Integrating social and financial returns. *California Management Review, 45*(4), 35–51.

Fama, E. F. (1980). Agency problems and the theory of the firm. *Journal of Political Economy, 88*(2), 288–307.

Fama, E. F., & Jensen, M. C. (1983). Agency problems and residual claims. *The Journal of Law and Economics, 26*(2), 327–349.

Fera, P., Pizzo, M., Vinciguerra, R. and Ricciardi, G. (2021). Sustainable corporate governance and new auditing issues: a preliminary empirical evidence on key audit matters. *Corporate Governance.* https://doi.org/10.1108/CG-09-2020-0427

Fich, E. M., Tran, A. L., & Walkling, R. A. (2013). On the importance of golden parachutes. *Journal of Financial and Quantitative Analysis,* 1717–1753. doi:10.1017/S002210901300063X

Fiori, G., & Tiscini R. (2014). *Economia Aziendale.* Milano: Egea.

Gainer, B. (2010). Corporate social responsibility. In R. Taylor (Ed.), *Third sector research* (pp. 187–200). New York: Springer.

Gair, C. (2002). A report from the good ship SROI. *San Francisco: The Roberts Foundation.* Retrieved from http://www.redf.org/download/sroi/goodshipsroi2.doc

Gallino, L. (2010). *L'impresa irresponsabile.* Turin: Giulio Einaudi Editore.

Gill, A. (2008). Corporate governance as social responsibility: A research agenda. *Berkeley Journal of International Law, 26,* 452.

Goodnight, G. T., & Green, S. (2010). Rhetoric, risk, and markets: The dot-com bubble. *Quarterly Journal of Speech, 96*(2), 115–140.

Gorzala, J. (2010). *The art of hostile takeover defence.* Hamburg: Igel Verlag.

Graves, B. (2005). Shareholder agreements. *Negotiating Major Business Agreements.* Retrieved from https://marcomm.mccarthy.ca/pubs/insight_paper_ver_two.pdf

Grossman, S. J., & Hart, O. D. (1980). Takeover bids, the free-rider problem, and the theory of the corporation. *The Bell Journal of Economics, 11*(1), 42–64.

Haid, M. (1997). *Incentive compensation and the market for corporate control: substitutive forces to discipline management of publicly held organizations in* the US: empirical evidence from the oil industry 1977–1994 (Vol. 16). Bern, Switzerland: Haupt.

Hart, O. D. (1983). The market mechanism as an incentive scheme. *The Bell Journal of Economics*, 14(2), 366–382.

Henderson, D. (2005). Turning Point: The role of business in the world of today. *Journal of Corporate Citizenship*, (17), 30–32. doi:10.9774/GLEAF.4700.2005.sp.00006

Hermalin, B. E. (2014). Transparency and corporate governance. In *Enterprise Law*. Edward Elgar Publishing. Available at: https://www.nber.org/system/files/working_papers/w12875/w12875.pdf

Heron, R. A., & Lie, E. (2006). On the use of poison pills and defensive payouts by takeover targets. *The Journal of Business*, 79(4), 1783–1807.

Hopkins, M. (2012). *Corporate social responsibility and international development: Is business the solution?*. London: Earthscan.

Jensen, M. C. (1986). Agency costs of free cash flow, corporate finance, and takeovers. *The American Economic Review*, 76(2), 323–329.

Jensen, M. C., & Meckling, W. H. (1976). Theory of the firm: Managerial behavior, agency costs and ownership structure. *Journal of Financial Economics*, 3(4), 305–360.

Kandel, E., Massa, M., & Simonov, A. (2011). Do small shareholders count?. *Journal of Financial Economics*, 101(3), 641–665.

King, M., & Roell, A. (1988). Insider trading. *Economic Policy*, 3(6), 163–193.

Lin, L., Ji, Z., He, S., & Zhu, Z. (2012, June). A crown jewel defense strategy based particle swarm optimization. In *2012 IEEE Congress on Evolutionary Computation* (pp. 1–6). IEEE.

Lombardo, G., Mazzocchetti, A., Rapallo, I., Tayser, N., & Cincotti, S. (2019). Assessment of the economic and social impact using SROI: An application to sport companies. *Sustainability*, 11(13), 3612.

Marris, R. (1963). A model of the 'managerial' enterprise. *The Quarterly Journal of Economics*, 77(2), 185–209.

Monks, R. A. G., & Minow, N. (2001). *Corporate governance*, 2nd edn. Oxford: Blackwell.

Mulgan, R. (2000). Accountability: An ever-expanding concept?. *Public Administration*, 78(3), 555–573. doi: 10.1111/1467-9299.00218

Myers, S. C., & Majluf, N. S. (1984). Corporate financing and investment decisions when firms have information that investors do not have. *Journal of Financial Economics*, 13(2), 187–221.

Norman, W., & MacDonald, C. (2004). Getting to the bottom of 'triple bottom line.' *Business ethics quarterly*, 14(2), 243–262.

Peters, T. (1990). Get innovative or get dead. *California Management Review*, 33(1).

Pistor, K. (1999). Codetermination: A sociopolitical model with governance externalities. In M. M. Blair and M. J. Roe (eds.), *Employees and corporate governance* (pp.163–191). Washington, D.C.: Brookings Institution Press.

Porta, R. L., Lopez-de-Silanes, F., Shleifer, A., & Vishny, R. W. (1998). Law and finance. *Journal of Political Economy, 106*(6), 1113–1155.

Porta, R. L., Lopez-de-Silanes, F., Shleifer, A., & Vishny, R. (2000). Investor protection and corporate governance. *Journal of Financial Economics, 58*(1–2), 3–27. doi: 10.1016/S0304-405X(00)00065-9.

Ramaswamy, V., Ueng, C. J., & Carl, L. (2008). Corporate governance characteristics of growth companies: An empirical study. *Academy of Strategic Management Journal, 12*, 21–33.

Rappaport, A. (1986). *Creating shareholder value: The new standard for business performance.* New York: Free Press.

Ravenscraft, D. J., & Scherer, F. M. (1987). Life after takeover. *The Journal of Industrial Economics, 36*(2), 147–156.

Shahin, A., & Zairi, M. (2007). Corporate governance as a critical element for driving excellence in corporate social responsibility. *International Journal of Quality & Reliability Management, 24*(7), 753–770. doi: 10.1108/0265671071 0774719

Shleifer, A., & Vishny, R. W. (1986). Large shareholders and corporate control. *Journal of political economy, 94*(3, Part 1), 461–488.

Shleifer, A., & Vishny, R. W. (1997). A survey of corporate governance. *The Journal of Finance, 52*(2), 737–783.

Slaper, T. F., & Hall, T. J. (2011). The triple bottom line: What is it and how does it work. *Indiana Business Review, 86*(1), 4–8.

Spiller, S. A. (2011). Opportunity cost consideration. *Journal of Consumer Research, 38*(4), 595–610. doi:10.1086/660045.

Tuan, L. T. (2012). Corporate social responsibility, ethics, and corporate governance. *Social Responsibility Journal, 8*(4), 547–560. doi:10.1108/174 71111211272110

Tuggle, C. S., Sirmon, D. G., Reutzel, C. R., & Bierman, L. (2010). Commanding board of director attention: Investigating how organizational performance and CEO duality affect board members' attention to monitoring. *Strategic Management Journal, 31*(9), 946–968.

Tullock, G. (1993). *Rent Seeking.* Hants, England: Edward Elgar.

Vagadia, B. (2014). Corporate governance. In Bharat Vagadia (Ed.), *Enterprise Governance. Driving Enterprise Performance Through Strategic Alignment* (pp. 209–257). Berlin: Springer-Verlag Berlin Heidelber. doi:10.1 007/978-3-642-38589-6_5.

Wagner, H. E. (1991). The open corporation. *California Management Review, 33*(4), 46–60.

Welford, R. (2007). Corporate governance and corporate social responsibility: Issues for Asia. *Corporate Social Responsibility and Environmental Management, 14*(1), 42–51.

2 Corporate Governance Systems in Capitalist Countries

2.1 Corporate Governance Theories

Among the main theories that offer very broad visions of the relationships among strategy, ownership and governance as well as the operational context of organisation, we can identify several theoretical approaches that allowed the development of CG throughout the years.

2.1.1 Managerial Approach

The theory developed by Chandler (1962, 1977, 1992) laid the basis for the origin and development of large managerial enterprise[1] in different sectors and countries during the nineteenth and twentieth centuries. In particular, Chandler's theory highlights a significant relationship between some context variables and the business strategy. In fact, it shows that large managerial enterprises only spread in the United States when, at the end of the nineteenth century, the communication and transport networks allowed the flow of resources to move between the productive and commercial units scattered throughout the territory. Furthermore, the theory indicates that the managerial enterprises are able to increase and subsequently prosper only if they are operating in sectors (i.e. oil, food and chemical), which provide them with the opportunity to obtain large economies of scale, scope and transaction, and if they are able to invest a high level of financial resources in large production plants and in an efficient distribution and marketing network, operating at both national and international levels. However, all these tasks, especially in production and marketing activities, need to be effectively coordinated by the management.

In addition, Chandler highlights the fact that each country has unique social, economic, historical and jurisdictional features that can influence both the ownership and managerial structures of the large

DOI: 10.4324/9781003225805-2

modern industrial enterprise and their purposes. In fact, in the United States, the separation between ownership and control determines the increase of professional managers who vigorously aim at improving the growth of the American industrial system. In the United Kingdom, on the other hand, large companies are still governed by their founders or the main shareholders, who favour the reach of profits in the short term to the detriment of medium-long term investments, which are instrumental in growth and competition. In Germany, professional managers make the necessary investments to exploit economies of scale and scope, while simultaneously, seeking close collaborations in order to establish cartels and agreements between competitors. Consequently, within the ownership structure of these companies, powerful banks play a central decisional role.

2.1.2 The 'Law and Finance' Approach

According to the law and finance approach (Porta, Lopez-de-Silanes, Shleifer, & Vishny, 1998, 1999), recently developed by economists and jurists, the legal context exerts a strong influence on the ownership and governance structure of companies. More specifically, in regard to the level of protection granted by the legal system to investors and on the level of effectiveness of its rules, CG codes[2] inspired by common law principles grant investors the highest protection, while codes belonging to the German and Scandinavian tradition have an intermediate level of protection. Sarkar analyses quantitatively a longitudinal dataset over a long time span (1970–2005) related to four OECD countries, such as the United Kingdom, United States, France and Germany, synthesising that France and Germany (civil law countries) were able to provide better protection to minority shareholders, while the United Kingdom and United States (common law countries) were able to protect creditors, especially in regard to insolvency (Sarkar & Singh, 2010:).

On the other hand, regarding the effectiveness of the legal system in enforcing the rules contained therein, the legal systems of the German and Scandinavian tradition, inspired by civil law principles, show the highest values of efficiency, while countries based on common law principles are characterised by intermediate to low level of efficiency. Regarding the latter (medium to low level of law enforcement), there are rules that constrain the behaviour of managers in the distribution and retention of profits produced by companies thus, it is primarily those rules that consequently strictly limit high-concentration ownership.

2.1.3 The Contingency Approach

This theory states that the ownership structure of a company must be designed according to the strategy it pursues. More specifically, the proprietary rights must be allocated according to a contingency logic aimed at minimising the sum of the transaction and management costs of the proprietary rights (Hansmann, 1988, 1996).

In regards to the first point, giving ownership rights to categories of subjects who have market relations with the company allows the elimination of the potential conflict of interest between buyers and sellers, which determines a large part of the market negotiation costs (Zattoni, 2011).

This conflict of interest is particularly high in the presence of a high *ex-ante* and *ex-post* market power (lock-in), and high information asymmetry. However, the allocation of ownership rights, in addition to solving some contractual issues, generates some costs that are particularly significant when shareholders cannot easily control managers, make firm and rational decisions and therefore, bear the business risk.

2.1.4 The Transaction Costs Theory

According to this theoretical approach, there is a clear relationship between the ownership and governance structure of a company and its strategic choices. In particular, an efficient company must adopt the form of governance that better allows the minimisation of the transaction costs incurred in managing the relationship with its stakeholders (Williamson, 1975, 1981).

Three types of transaction costs can be identified in the real market:

- search and information costs (related to the search of relevant information in order for the transaction to take place. The stockbroker's fee represents a valid example of information transaction cost);
- bargaining costs (refer to the reach of an agreement among the parties involved in drawing up a contract);
- policing and enforcement costs (aim at ensuring that the parties in the contract do not default on the terms of the contract. Lawyers' fees can be considered as a typical demonstrative example of such costs).

Overall, transaction costs are particularly high in the case of transactions uncertain, frequent and, above all, if they require specific investments. The market, hierarchy and hybrid form of company governance have a different ability to incentivize efficient behaviour and to adequately control the onset of opportunistic behaviours. The market is characterised by the presence of strong incentives for opportunistic behaviour and therefore represents the most efficient solution when the identity of the contractors is irrelevant. The hierarchy has diametrically opposed characteristics representing the most efficient solution when the transaction is particularly complex and involves the support of high-specific investments. Finally, the 'hybrid' form is characterised by an average intensity of incentives and administrative control, and it represents the optimal solution when the transaction requires medium specificity of the resources needed, it does not show frequent changes. According to Coase (1937), however, the cost for organising transactions within firms should be compared with the cost incurred in organising transactions through markets. In addition, the author affirms that the existence of firms is linked to the presence of transaction costs.

2.1.5 The Theory of Property Rights

This theoretical perspective affirms the existence of a direct relationship between the strategic choices made by the company and the efficient allocation of ownership rights. In particular, the ownership of a resource assigns to its owner the right to influence its allocation and the method of use. Ownership is identified in this case with the possession of the residual rights of control, and therefore, the right to exclude other people from the possibility to use the owned resource (Grossman & Hart, 1986). Ownership of a resource is particularly important when that resource is specific and rare; therefore, the company that makes important investment in a resource should own it.

2.1.6 The Theory of Institutional Asset

The theory of the institutional asset argues that there is a close relationship between the company's strategy, the distribution of proprietary rights and its governance structure. In particular, the identification of the type of activities carried out by a company determines the criticality of the contribution provided by the various stakeholders.

The stakeholders who provide the critical contributions must receive the ownership rights or, at least, their interests ought to be protected (Zattoni, 2011).

The criticality of the various contributions given by the stakeholders is closely related to the characteristics assumed by the contractual relationship that binds the stakeholder to the company. In this context, the extent of contractual costs, corporate risk and the impact of the contribution of stakeholders on corporate performance are extremely important. Therefore, the task of the company is mainly that of avoiding the reduction of the commitment of its stakeholders or, even worse, their abandonment of the company that could severely jeopardise its survival.

2.2 International Models of CG

The theoretical excursus provided should be interpreted as the theoretical foundation on which different countries have shaped and built different CG structures to choose from. This choice is widely influenced by the historical, cultural, economic and geographical context where the company operates. In addition, the corporate (Enron, WorldCom, Global Crossing, Vivendi, Tyco, Cirio, Parmalat) and financial scandals (Subprime loans crisis) that occurred in the past twenty years has definitely highlighted the weakness of the internal and external control systems in fighting against the unfair consequences of senior management's behaviour, which consequently led to the loss of trust among savers. Hence, the awareness of a national and international commitment to establish precise rules of good CG aimed at reducing the international gap between global markets and systems of CG and external supervision.

In recent years, the establishment of the global competition network has led numerous countries and supranational organisations to promote regulatory interventions on CG in order to guarantee international convergence, communication and control in favour of shareholders and stakeholders, and flexibility of structures, thanks to the possibility to choose between different governance models, different countries tend not to change their models but to improve them based on the skills acquired. The debate on the international convergence towards a specific system of CG is still ongoing due to the fact that despite the thrust given by the globalisation of financial markets and the homogenisation of national cultures and regulations, the differences among the various models still remain evident. Therefore, it emerges that there is no absolute superior system, as each is specific to each national context.

The CG structures and rules can be introduced by the national legislator or by private initiative based on the dominant legal regime.

In this regard, we can distinguish between *common law* and *civil law* countries. In the first category of countries, the predominant source of law is jurisprudence due to the fact that there is no written law while the Supervisory Bodies of the Stock Exchanges have to draft binding recommendations for admission to listing. The civil law system is applied to Anglo-Saxon countries that are characterised by extensive use of the financial market and the prevalence of large companies with pulverised ownership where the problem of the separation between ownership and control incurs more frequently as shareholders are not incentivised for controlling the managing so that it pursues their interests.

In civil law countries, on the other hand, laws represent the reference framework to be followed in order not to violate the interests of shareholders and other stakeholders while the financial market is not very relevant as the ownership is often transferred through agreements between the parties. In essence, the main difference between the two regimes lies in the different weights exerted by the financial market that entails a different degree of intervention by public authorities and supervisory bodies. Therefore, regulations will be more present in countries where the financial market is less developed and cannot guarantee due protections for shareholders and other stakeholders.

Different factors can influence the structure of different CG systems including:

- ability of the financial market to attract savings;
- role played by the Banks;
- co-management of companies by different types of stakeholders, such as workers (i.e. Germany);
- separation (closeness) between ownership and management.

2.2.1 *Outsider and Insider System*

Based on the type of monitoring, external or internal, over the management's activities, a CG system can be defined as either *outsider* or *insider* system. In the first type, the monitoring of the managers' activities is external, more specifically, is implemented by the market, while in the second type, managers are monitored internally by the main stakeholders.

The *outsider system*, also called market-oriented system, is developed in common law legal systems (Anglo-Saxon countries), characterised by high protection of minority shareholders and corporate creditors. Companies, also defined as public companies, as they are large in size with highly fractional ownership, require an efficient financial market to carry out their activities and achieve their business targets. The stock markets must be well developed and include a high capacity to attract resources in order to facilitate the transactions of securities based on the information available on CG and company results. The limit of this model lies in the separation between ownership and control. As investors are only interested in quickly and effortlessly obtaining profits and, above all, not willing to bear the cost of controls, managers hold a strong discretional power as they can have direct access to company information and thus pursue their own interests and not the stakeholders'. In this case, management control can only be carried out through the judgement given by the financial market which tends to incentivize companies to fight against excessive discretionary power of managers through remuneration systems linked to company performance. In addition, in the outsider system, the duration of managers' contract tends to be short in order to avoid an excessive acquisition of information, which can lead to great difficulties in monitoring and controlling their activities. In conclusion, this system assumes a positive role in economies with strong financial development due to the power given to specialised managers who are not subjected to direct control over their work.

The *insider system* is based on the importance given to the relationship between the government, the industry and the banking system to achieve economic and social development. It tends to develop in civil law countries usually characterised by underdeveloped financial markets with a small number of shares traded daily. In this context, the task of the stock market is to keep the value of the securities high, also by resorting to the purchase of own shares. This behaviour model is the result of the economic and entrepreneurial national tradition aimed at consolidating the ownership structure. In addition, in the outsider system, there is no clear separation between ownership and control, as internal control is exercised by a small group of shareholders (blockholders), generally of a family or banking nature, which holds the control of the company through voting trust agreement or reciprocal and pyramidal shareholdings, therefore, hostile takeovers to replace the management are extremely difficult to accomplish. In the insider system of CG, managers have the arduous task of finding the right compromise in order to satisfy and balance the interests of majority and minority shareholders especially for the latter who have little decision-making power and their interests are unlikely to be well represented and protected.

Based on the historical and economic events that have occurred throughout the years in different countries, we can distinguish various types of insider systems, namely the Rhenish system; the Latin system and the system that is developing in transition economies (we may call it the *transition system*).

• The *Rhenish system* was originally developed in Germany, and then spread to the rest of Europe. This system is based on collaboration with stakeholders. More specifically, the Rhenish system is oriented towards the co-management of the company which is characterised by the active participation of banks and workers[3]. On the one hand, the top management has to coordinate the numerous corporate relationships that are based on mutual trust, reputation and corporate image. On the other hand, managers have to seek profitable and lasting collaborations in order to share economic risk and growth. The mandate of managers, most often elected by employees, is often multi-year and the control body has normally more members than the management team.

• The *Latin system* is developed in different European countries such as Italy, France, Belgium, Spain, Portugal and Greece. As in the Rhenish system, there are controlling shareholders in the Latin system, often represented by families, credit institutions or public bodies, with high strategic power guaranteed by voting agreements and share crossings. Therefore, banks and employees do not play a management role, as both are simple external stakeholders carrying out indecisive functions. Banks are simple lenders with only indirect influence on the decision-making process by limiting credit to the organisation, while employees can only be protected by the presence of trade unions. Thus, the Latin system can be considered as a combination between the Anglo-Saxon and the Rhenish model.

• The *transition system* is the last type of insider system of CG which has been developing in economies in transition[4] such as Russia and China. As in the Rhenish system, in the transition system, the financial market is weak and there are controlling shareholders who, given their position of supremacy, often abuse inside information, therefore, causing distorting effects on the capital market. In addition, in the transition insider system, investors' confidence is fed by cross-relations that the company can establish with other companies or banks and, above all, by the support given by political institutions.

2.2.2 *One-Tier and Two-Tier System*

The function of management and control functions can be led by either one (one-tier system) or two bodies (two-tier system).

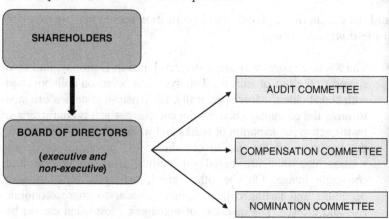

Figure 2.1 The *one-tier* corporate governance system.

In the *one-tier system*, also defined as the *monistic system*, the shareholders' meeting appoints both the administrative and control body which belongs to the administrative body as well. More specifically, the shareholders' meeting appoints the administrative body called the *board of directors* is composed of two types of directors: *executive directors* who manage the organisations (among them it can be appointed the general manager or Chief Executive Officer (CEO)) and *non-executive directors* who directly participate in the management of the organisations without a direct contact with the shareholders. In fact, the latter are also called outsider directors, because, unlike the executive directors, they do not own company shares, therefore, are able to guarantee an independent judgement based on rationality and fairness, avoiding the pursuit of egotistically driven interests (Figure 2.1).

The peculiarity of this CG system is the fact that the function of control and monitoring is only exercised internally by non-executive directors through three committees:

- compensation committee: calculates the salary of both managers and directors;
- nomination committee: recommends the potential directors to the shareholders' meeting;
- audit committee: controls and supervises the executive directors' activities.

Therefore, the role played by the non-executive directors is essential in the one-tier system, in fact, they have to be carefully selected by the shareholders' meeting and, above all, they have to show profession-alism and trustworthiness in order to complete their tasks.

Although the one-tier system is well spread in both United States and United Kingdom as it is based on the so-called trust[5] between the shareholders and the board of directors, there is a lot of criticism about this system. Firstly, the role of non-executive directors as con-trollers is accused of being not entirely impartial as they still belong to the board of directors, therefore, controllers and subjects being con-trolled belong to the same board. Secondly, the scarce quality of the information at the disposal of non-executive directors has also been criticised in comparison with the high quality and promptness of the information acquired by executive directors. Finally, there may be a limited tendency of the non-executive directors to contrast executive directors' choices as they both belong to the same board.

Within the *two-tier system*, also defined as the *dualistic system*, the administration and control function is exercised by two separate bodies; the *management board* that holds executive responsibilities and the *supervisory board* that is appointed by shareholders' meeting and, among its functions, it approves the financial statements and, above all, is entitled to appoint, control and remove members of the man-agement board. We can identify two types of dualistic CG systems: the vertical and horizontal systems. The difference between the two sys-tems stems from the subjects who are entitled to appoint the member of the management and the supervisory board.

In the vertical dualistic system, the general shareholders' meeting appoints the members of the supervisory boards who, in turn, appoint the members of the management board (Figure 2.2).

The vertical system was initially developed in Germany to introduce a control body that could, on the one hand, control the management of the company and, on the other hand, meet stakeholders' needs.

Conversely, in the horizontal dualistic system, the general share-holders' meeting appoints both members of the management and the supervisory board. In this CG model, typically developed in Italy and in small percentage in other countries, there is one fundamental rule that has to be followed: no one can be a member of either the su-pervisory board (*collegio sindacale*) or the management board (*Consiglio di amministrazione*) (Figure 2.3).

Over all, in the dualistic models, the management board's activities include the drafting and implementation of strategic plans. The Supervisory Board supervises the implementation of operational pro-grams and verifies the quality of the information and internal control system. In addition, the supervisory board can decide in place of

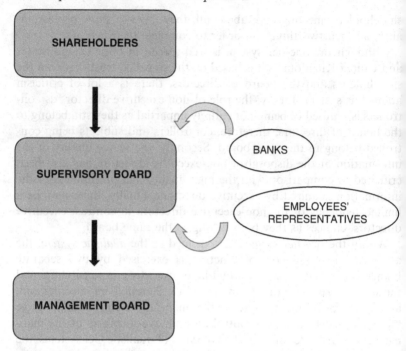

Figure 2.2 The *two-tier* (vertical) corporate governance system.

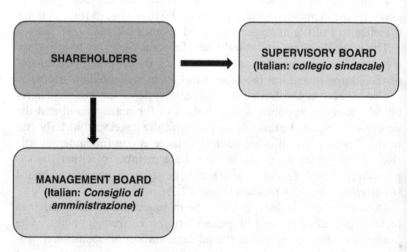

Figure 2.3 The *two-tier* (horizontal) corporate governance system.

unavailability of the general shareholders' meeting to decide especially in case-specific necessary skills (i.e. accounting knowledge for financial statements approval). The two-tier system is generally chosen in the case of generational transitions as the founding members have the possibility of joining the Supervisory Board and, therefore, supervise the management of their company. The criticism of the two-tier system is based on the fact that the supervisory board has to frequently authorise specific decisions taken by the management board which, therefore, hinders the smooth execution of activities.

In the following excerpts, after a brief introduction regarding the roots of the CG models mainly adopted in specific countries, different cases are presented in order to show the pragmatic applications of the CG models presented in theory so far.

2.3 The United States of America: The *One-Tier* System

Corporate governance in the United States is regulated by each federal state. Therefore, each organisation is subject to the law of the state where it has established its registered office and the choice regarding the state where to establish the company headquarters depends on the legal and tax advantages offered by each state. This creates fierce competition among the states in order to attract the largest number of companies. In regard to some aspects related to CG, US companies are all subject to federal legislation, which is valid in all states and to the rules of the stock markets where their securities are admitted to listing.

Modern large enterprise appeared in the US economic system at the end of the nineteenth century, when some innovations allowed companies to produce goods on a large scale, but also to effectively coordinate a large flow of productive resources located in different geographical areas. These innovations have strongly encouraged the productive concentration of many goods in a few large companies that, under an oligopoly regime, found themselves in a position to fix sales prices in order to maximise their profits. Between the end of the nineteenth and the beginning of the twentieth centuries, the US federal government enacted strict antitrust legislation[6] aimed at preventing, or at least severely hindering, collusive practices to the detriment of consumers.

In regard to the contractual relationships among companies, each company is responsible for a specific phase of the same supply chain, the US model has traditionally been characterised by the high vertical integration of large companies and the creation of short-term market relationships with suppliers.

In addition, the relationship between banks and companies was regulated by legislation that strictly supervised the functioning of the stock markets and the behaviour of financial intermediaries. In this regard, the Security and Exchange Commission (SEC) was established in 1947 in response to the Great Depression as a stock market supervisory body, which clearly separated the activity of credit management from that of direct acquisition of shares.

The CG model applied in the United States and also in Canada and Australia is identifiable as a managerial model due to its peculiarities as an outsider system (market oriented). This managerial model is characterised by the presence of public companies (the term public indicates that the stockholding belongs to public investors, therefore, companies are not state-owned), individual investors holding a small amount of shares who, being unable to impact on company's decisions, are only interested in achieving speculatively a capital gain in the short-run and not participating in shareholders' meetings.

The fragmented stockholding, combined with the rational disinterest of the shareholders in the management of the company, allows managers to determine the strategic direction of the company and control it without bearing the economic risk of the choices made and this creates a clear separation between ownership and control, arising enormous conflict between shareholders and managers (the agency problem). This conflictual situation leads to the bearing of the agency costs related to the delegation of the minority shareholders to managers who, in fact, act as agents of the owners by deciding which investments to make and how to finance them.

Managers have been increasingly influenced by institutional investors (mutual investment funds and pension funds) due to the growing propensity of private investors to entrust their savings to the management of specialised intermediaries. Unlike individual savers, specialised investors own significant stakes in the largest companies and therefore have the power to direct, or at least influence, the behaviour of managers towards the creation of share value. In the early nineties, institutional investors began to exert increasing pressure on the behaviour of top managers in order to push top management to lead the company in view of maximising share value. However, *Enron, WorldCom, Global Crossing, Qwest Communication International, All First, Rite Aid, Republic Securities and* many other scandals have created distrust among investors in the American stock market. In response to these scandals, few regulations were introduced in order to contain the spread of negative effects of the scandals.

The pillars of the current 'US framework' on CG are the Sarbanes and Oxley Act of 2002 and the SEC and New York Stock Exchange

(NYSE or *Big Board*) Regulations on CG developed throughout the years. In response to the financial and economic crisis incurred in 2008/ 2009, the Dodd-Frank Act was issued in 2020 with the aim of re-structuring the supervisory framework of the financial system by in-cluding all public companies in the federal regulation of CG. In addition, the Dodd-Frank established two agencies, namely, the *Financial Stability Oversight Council* and the *Office of Financial Research* to keep the financial system in the United States balanced and stable by controlling the stock markets and, above all, protect consumers and investors.

Overall, the main governance requirements outlined in this frame-work include a board of directors in which the majority of the direc-tors has to be non-executive and independent (the number of outsider executives is stated in the governance documents of the company), the presence of at least three committees at the board level (internal control, remuneration, nominee), composed of independent directors who do not play an active role in the governance of the company due to their limited information available and commitment as they already have other roles such as bank managers, partners of professional firms working with the company. In addition, the pressure exerted on di-rectors by the CEO can consistently influence the board of directors (both insider and outsider directors) and, therefore, diminish the power of the entire board. This depletion of power of the administra-tive body tends to progressively direct the *one-tier* CG system, well established in the United States, towards the *two-tier* system that characterises the European model.

2.3.1 Case Study: Ford Motor Company

The car manufacturer was founded in the State of Michigan in 1903 by Henry Ford, who is known for having introduced for the first time the assembly line and conveyor belt, later implemented by plentiful other companies (this phenomenon was soon defined as Fordism). The core business of Ford is passenger cars rather than industrial vehicles. In fact, approximately 170 models have been produced since the estab-lishment of the company. The enormous success allowed Ford to ex-pand worldwide, opening numerous branches in Europe, Asia, Africa and South America and, above all, the acquisition of other car man-ufacturers such as Land Rover, Jaguar, Aston Martin and Volvo.

However, the financial and economic crisis that hit the globe in 2008 forced the implementation of a plan called *The Way Forward,* which consisted of selling all the car manufacturers previously acquired and dismissing plentiful jobs in order to face the losses recorded.

Ford Motor Company is listed at the New York Stock Exchange and adopts the *one-tier* CG model.

The framework for governance of Ford Motor Company is based on CG principles and the charters of the five committees established to assist the board of directors:

- *Audit Committee* supports the directors of company regarding accounting and keeping high quality and reliability of financial reporting;
- *Compensation, Talent and Culture Committee* helps the board draft compensation programs for talented executives;
- *Sustainability and Innovation Committee* is responsible for evaluating and advising the company in regard to innovations that pursue environmental and social sustainability;
- *Finance Committee* is responsible for the strategic management of the financial matters of the Company including drafting policies and implementing practices;
- *Nominating and Governance Committee* helps the board select potential candidates for all directorships and it also evaluates and recommends the board in regard to governance policies and procedures.

The Board of Directors, whose members are elected in annual shareholder's general meeting, revise the CG principles and monitor the performance of the CEO in order to assure that the needs and interests of the shareholders are adequately met.

The independence of the majority of directors is defined in the guidelines issued by Ford in accordance with the NYSE rules.[7]

2.4 Germany: The *Two-Tier* System

The structure of the German industrial system is represented by a very large number of medium-sized companies (the so-called *Mittelstand*), characterised by governance models that are not particularly sophisticated, the Limited Liability Company (LLC) or *Gesellschaft mit Beschrankter Haftung* (GmbH) controlled by individuals or family. Therefore, the joint-stock company tends to be limited to larger companies. At the start of the new millennium, GmnH were about 600.000, while the joint-stock companies or *Aktiengesellschaft* (AG) were just over 3500 of which one-fifth listed, which show, in terms of ownership structures and control models, some specific characteristics such as the extensive presence in almost all the listed AGs of significant blockholders (individual-family founders, private organisations and banks) with stakes exceeding 25% of the share capital. This strict control of the company by very few shareholders was allowed using different tools, such as cross holdings[8] (Adams, 1999), Stock pyramids[9] and Dual-class equity[10] (Bebchuk, Kraakman, & Triantis, 2000). The combined use of stock pyramids and cross-shareholdings generally strengthened by *interlocking* (the reciprocal presence of directors on the boards of companies) has helped to further strengthen the compactness of German capitalism. It is therefore, precisely on these intertwining, that the action of regulators has been concentrated in recent years, as well as on other instruments traditionally used in order to strengthen the position of controlling shareholders, including multiple voting shares (which has no longer been possible to issue since 1998), the shareholders' agreements (not frequent, and now obligatorily to be indicated in the annual report). However, all these tools represent an effective reminder of the cooperative/collusive nature of German capitalism.

Despite the fact that the most recent legislative pressures in terms of national governance codes have heavily affected this situation, a whole series of events testify to the tenacious persistence of the 'German model' (the so-called Deutschland AG) of governance of large companies.

The financial resources to support future investments come largely from corporate self-financing. This explains the lack of a dynamic and large stock market and the presence of controlling shareholders linked to each other, therefore, very rare hostile takeovers. In fact, the typical institutional structure model of large companies operating in the German economic systems is represented by a strong emphasis on relations between industrial and financial companies and the presence of a coalition of controlling shareholders. Among them, banks play a crucial role in particular in the so-called *big three,* Deutsche Bank, Dresdner Bank and Commerzbank, which exercises pressure on companies through the proxy voting mechanism.

In Germany, joint-stock companies must adopt the *two-tier* CG system represented by a board of directors consisting of two distinct and hierarchically subordinate bodies: the supervisory board and the management board. The internal organisation of joint-stock companies is determined by German law with mandatory rules regarding the composition and appointment of the bodies as well as the division of competencies among them.

More specifically:

- *general shareholders' meeting* does not have general competence, it deliberates only on specific matters defined by the law expressly indicated by the law or articles of its association. It also decides on the appointment and dismissal of the shareholders' representatives in the *Aufsichtsrat* (supervisory board), the allocation of budget profits, amendments to the articles of association, capital increases and reductions and the dissolution of the company. It is also called to approve the work performed by the *Vorstand* (board of directors) and the *Aufsichtsrat*. Shareholders have the right to obtain from the Vorstand all information useful for the conscious exercise of voting on the items on the agenda;

- *supervisory board (Aufsichtsrat),* which consists of non-executive board members, is responsible for the company's general policy by making fundamental choices regarding the company's life and exercising control over Vorstand's activity. It meets normally every quarter and may appoint a chairman's committee that meets more frequently. This body is composed of three members or a multiple of three up to a maximum of twenty-one members, whose mandate cannot be longer than four years. The body is characterised by the fact that it is composed of shareholders' representatives appointed by the general shareholders' meeting and workers' representatives appointed under the provisions of the law (*Mitbestimmungsgesetz Act*) on 'co-management or co-determination' *(Mitbestimmung)* according to which listed companies employing between 501 and 2000 employees must have a supervisory board that consists of employee representatives representing one-third of the board, while in case of more than 2000 employee, the supervisory board must contain half of employees representatives. According to the OECD, in the case of 'companies not subject to co-determination the Supervisory Board should usually consist of three members. The articles of association may establish a higher number of board members which, commensurate with the registered capital of the company concerned, may amount to a maximum of 9, 15, or 21 members' (2021: 178). Overall, listed companies in many cases have CEOs and experts especially in the financial field (auditors or accountants).

- *management board (Vorstand)* is entrusted with the management and the judicial and extrajudicial representation of the company and it functions through executive board members holding decisional power (OECD, 2021). Therefore, they do not act as 'assistants' of their president, the CEO (*Vorstandsvorsitzender*), appointed by the supervisory board (*Aufsichtsrat*). The members of the Vorstand, whose number is fixed by the articles of association, may not be shareholders and are appointed by the *Aufsichtsrat* with a two-thirds majority, from which they can be dismissed in case of serious reasons such as a grave breach of duty. The members of the Vorstand stay on duty for five years and can be re-elected only once. The role of CEO does not require any particular legal specificities and is considered as *primus inter pares* in order to highlight the lack of supremacy in comparison with the other executive members.

In principle, the directors are exempt from liability when they act in execution of valid shareholders' meeting deliberations. Moreover, when it is reasonably foreseeable that the execution of valid shareholders' meeting resolutions may cause damage to the company, the law attributes to the directors the power and duty to challenge those damaging resolutions, with the consequence that they cannot be exempt from liability in the event of the execution of such deliberations.

Overall, the German model of CG has been questioned especially in regard to:

- low frequency of supervisory board meetings;
- the quality of the information provided by the company's management to the supervisory board, which is in many cases, fragmented and scarcely exhaustive;
- the members of the supervisory board who, very often, hold similar positions in other companies and consequently, their ability to effectively control the performance of the company is reduced;
- the fact that in companies with a number of employees exceeding 2000 units, 50% of the total number of supervisory board members is appointed by employees, it has not proved its capability of adequately performing its control functions due to the poor-quality information provided.

2.4.1 Case Study: Hugo Boss

Hugo Boss is a luxury fashion design listed public company founded in Metzingen in 1924 by Hugo Ferdinand Boss. As a member of the Nazi Party, the founder initially produced and sold Nazi uniforms. However, after his death and the end of World War II, the core business of the company shifted towards men's suits. After forty years,

Hugo Boss decided to offer women's clothes and at the beginning of the new millennium, also children's clothing, becoming one of the most important global fashion houses with more than one thousand shops worldwide.

Hugo Boss went public in 1988 and is currently listed in the Frankfurt Stock Exchange. The Shareholder structure (70,400,00 of shares) is composed of more than 80% of the shares in *free float* (belonging to institutional investors located in Europe and the United States), 2% owned by the company itself and the remaining 15% belongs to two Italy companies, PFC Srl. and Zignago Holding S.p.A.

According to section 289f of the German Commercial Codes (HGB), each listed company has to issue a statement on CG which has to include three main pieces of information: a declaration of compliance with German Commercial Codes, information regarding the corporate practices and the functioning of both Management and Supervisory Board.

In regard to the declaration of compliance, Hugo Boss issues the declaration of compliance with the recommendations of the amended version (2017) of the 'German Corporate Governance Code' defining, however, the exceptions from the recommendation.

Regarding information on corporate practices, Hugo Boss carries out corporate actions responsible under a social and environmental point of view and, nonetheless, maintains respect to its employees. All these elements are considered as fundamental drivers of high competitiveness and success in the long run.

Within the managing board, composed of the spokesperson and the board members, every member has equal rights in carrying out the Managing Board's tasks including the definition and implementation of corporate strategy, corporate finance and risk management. In addition, the managing board decides on the sales network and product sourcing and it is also responsible for the presentation of the company to both media and capital market.

Regarding the supervisory board, Hugo Boss pays careful attention to skills and independence of its supervisory board members. In fact, out of twelve members, six of them are employees' representatives in order to guarantee employees' representativeness within the controlling body.

In order to conduct their activities, the supervisory board benefits from five committees whose chairs regularly report to the supervisory board:

- *audit committee,* composed of six members appointed by the supervisory board, is responsible for the internal control systems, the risk management, the internal auditing and drafting the yearly financial statements;

• *personnel committee* consists of five other members chosen by the Supervisory Board and the Chairman of the Supervisory Board. Overall, the personnel committee decides on the contracts of the Managing Board members but not in regard to their salary, which is a specific responsibility of the full Supervisory Board;

• *working committee* consists of five other members chosen by the Supervisory Board and the Chairman of the Supervisory Board. Overall, the working committee provides support and assistance to the Chairman of the supervisory board. In particular, it organises the meetings of the supervisory board and monitors duties between meetings;

• *nomination committee* is composed of two members appointed by the representatives of the shareholders on the Supervisory Board. It identifies potential candidates for the election of shareholder representatives to the Supervisory Board at the annual shareholders' meeting.

• *mediation Committee* has the only duty of submitting proposals of members of the managing board in cases the previous proposal has not reached the required statutory majority. It is composed of four members: The Chairman of the Supervisory Board, the Deputy Chairman of the Supervisory Board, one member elected by the employees' and shareholders' representatives on the Supervisory Board.

2.5 Japan: The *Hybrid* System

In the Japanese business model, institutions, corporate ownership structures, financial market structure and governance models are combined based on the established patterns in the medium-long term. The success of the large Japanese companies, based on the so-called Asian model is characterised by:

• the development of a unique corporate structure called *keiretsu*,[11] a corporate group where each organisation member operates in a different business sector but linked to one another through cross-holdings without the control of a holding company;

• the presence of a *bank* belonging to the group, being both creditor and shareholders and its own representative in the board of directors (bank-based financed);

• the presence of a strong *social integration* of workers who are able to develop virtuous relationships leading to high performance for each group member.

Post World War II, the introduction of few reforms strongly reduced the possibility to operate cross-holdings among enterprises and, above all, between organisations and banks. The purpose of these reforms was that of implementing an 'Americanisation' of the Japanese corporate structure where organisations would obtain financial resources through the stock market rather than the internal bank system acting also as shareholders. It is important to note that this new system did not take off as expected. In fact, the high presence of cross-holdings among organisations belonging to different business sectors and the imposing role played by banks as main creditors of the organisations highlighted the continuity of the previous model. However, the Japanese banking crisis that occurred in the 1990s, mainly attributed to the deregulation of an increasing capital market characterised by an inadequate regulatory framework (Kanaya & Woo, 2000), strongly diminished the possibility for Japanese organisations to be internally financed by the banking system. Therefore, there was a sharp and sudden fall in shares owned by banks and, simultaneously, an increase in the usage of a direct financing system, the stock market.

In regard to CG, Japan, Italy and Portugal are the only countries that offer the possibility to select among different models. More specifically, 'Japan amended its Company Act in 2014 to introduce a new type of board structure, a company with an audit and supervisory committee, besides models providing for a board with statutory auditor and a company with three committees' (OECD, 2021: 139). More specifically, the three CG models to choose from are:

- *model with statutory auditors:* the management of the company is led by the board of directors, which is composed of at least one executive director and non-executive directors. The supervisory function is carried out by the statutory audit group, which is composed of auditors (*Kansayaku*), appointed by the shareholders' meeting, who have to legally check on directors' activities. According to the Act No. 86 of 2005 (The Companies Act), the audit committee (the statutory auditors) in large companies has to be composed, for at least half, of external auditors (not previously worked in the company neither as employees nor as executive directors);
- *model with three committees:* there is a sharp separation between the management and supervisory function. The former is appointed to the executive officers of the board of directors, while the latter is carried out by independent directors (outside directors) through three specific committees composed mostly of outside directors: nomination, remuneration and audit committee.

-*model with an audit and supervisory committee:* the shareholders' meeting establishes the audit and supervisory committee that has to be composed of at least three directors, of which the majority must be outside directors. In addition to the functions carried out by the statutory auditors, at the general shareholders' meeting, the audit and supervisory committee gives an opinion regarding the election and compensations of the members of the board of directors.

In Japan, there are two main sources of CG rules: *regulatory and non-regulatory sources.* The first group belongs The Companies Act (Act No. 86 of 2005) which applies whether the company is listed or not, and it defines the rights and obligations of the management and the disclosure of information; The Financial Instruments and Exchange Act (Act. No. 25 of 1948) which requires organisations to draft and timely submit reports on internal control activities carried, securities issued, and material information provided; The regulations issued by the Tokyo Stock Exchange (TSE) regarding the obligation of listed companies to draft and submit CG reports and select at least one 'independent officer' (defined as either outside director or statutory auditor). Regarding the non-regulatory source of CG rules such as the internal regulations issued by the company, the Japan's Corporate Governance Code aimed at listed companies provides the main principles for an effective CG. Finally, the regulations issued by some investor groups such as the Pension Fund Association regarding the exercise of proxy voting.

2.5.1 Case Study: Nikon Corporation

Nikon (*Nippon Kōgaku Kōgyō Kabushikigaisha*) was founded by Koyata Iwasaki in 1917, it was renamed as *Nikon Corporation* (or simply Nikon) in 1988, and nowadays, it is the world's eighth-largest electronic equipment producer. Nikon belongs to the *keiretsu* Mitsubishi group and is listed in the Tokyo Stock Exchange showing a percentage of 20–30% of foregoing shareholding.[12]

Among the three CG models available, Nikon adopted the model with audit and supervisory committee. The board of directors must have at least two external directors which, in 2021 has five external directors, checks on directors' activities and decides on the matters defined by the articles of incorporation of Nikon, and more generally, by laws and regulations. Directors composing the board have to be skilful and experienced in regard to finance, accounting and legal matters while other directors must have extensive knowledge regarding the core business of Nikon.

The audit and supervisory committee is an independent body that audits and oversees the activities of directors. According to the articles of incorporation, the audit and supervisory committee is to have no more than five members with the majority of independent external directors particularly knowledgeable regarding financial and accounting matters. Nikon's board of directors benefits from the two additional committees; the nomination and compensation committee. The former is fully responsible for defining the criteria for the election and dismissal of the CEO, president and directors, while the latter is responsible for directors' compensation especially for the part linked with Nikon's performance. Both nomination and compensation committees are composed of mostly external directors among whom there is the committees' chairperson.

2.6   France: The Choice Between *One* and *Two-Tier* System

French industrial capitalism went through two distinct phases throughout the twentieth century, both shaped the structures that still characterise large industrial companies today. The first phase, which lasted until the second post-war period, saw the establishment of the family business model operating in the typical sectors of the second industrial revolution such as iron and steel, mechanical, textiles and large-scale distribution. The low penetration of the German financing model and the limited use of the stock market contributed to maintaining the high concentration of control of large companies in the hands of the founders or their families.

In the second phase, following the Second World War, the French government undertook direct intervention policies in the industrial sector through the nationalisation of some of the most important companies and through substantial interference in the economic field that, in fact, substantially limited the development of capitalism. This second phase, concurred with the expansion of technologically advanced sectors through 'representative' public and private groups, ended rather abruptly around the mid-1980s when an intense privatisation policy took place, lasting until the early years of the new millennium. The wave of privatisation spread over the consolidated French industry, divided into large state-owned enterprises run by generalist managers from large polytechnic schools and public administration, and large private family-run companies. The privatisation process, beyond the short-term financial effects on the French state budget, had an important and visible effect, in the medium term, on the ownership and control of the major French corporations that have been greatly influenced by the growing use of the shareholder value philosophy, the increase in the frequency and volume of IPOs[13] and by the rising the importance of institutional investors in corporate ownership. However, it should be emphasised that the French government still stubbornly persists, in a line of continuity with the past, to show non-superficial interference with the private sector, especially sectors considered strategic, such as the energy sector. Therefore, the current structure of the major French companies is characterised by a marked decline in direct ownership of the government, a rather constant relevance of individual and family ownership and, on the other hand, an increasing presence of institutional investors operating in a fairly dynamic stock market as a substitute means to obtain financing outside the banking system.

Companies can opt for different corporate forms, more specifically:

- *Société anonyme* or SA (company limited by shares) is the corporate form mainly adopted by listed companies;
- *Société par actions simplifiée* or SAS (a simplified company limited by shares) represents a flexible corporate form chosen by wholly-owned French subsidiaries of not listed companies;
- *Société à responsabilité limitée* or SARL (limited liability company) is generally applied to small and medium-sized organisation.
- -*Société en commandite par actions* or SCA (partnership) is characterised by the presence of both general partners (*commandités*) and limited partners (*commanditaires*). Some key decisions need the unanimous approval of the general partners. The voluntary and non-legally binding French Corporate Governance Code (*Afep-Medef Code*) does not list shares issued by companies with this corporate form.
- *Société européenne* or SE (European stock company) is adopted by few large listed companies as this form is more flexible than SA as it allows the transfer of the registered office within the EU.

The French law allows companies to opt for two CG models: the one-tier system, similar to the German model and two-tier system, more similar to the Anglo-Saxon model (Millet-Reyes & Zhao, 2010). Within the one-tier model or monistic CG model, the direction (executive directors) and supervision (non-executive directors) are exercised by one management body through the support of different committees focused on specific matters such as audit, compensation and nomination. In the two-tier or dualistic CG model, the directors and the supervisory board are two separate bodies.

The French law leaves the power to decide the methods of administration to the statutory autonomy of the company; however, in case the CG structure is not defined in statute, the one-tier model applies. The management function of the company is exercised through:

- the *board of directors,* who are responsible for the definition and implementation of the company's strategy under a social and environmental point of view;
- the *chairperson* of the board of directors, responsible for the organisation and direction and supervision of the board of directors' work;
- the *CEO*, responsible for general management of the company and its representation to third parties. The CEO could also exercise the function of the *chairperson* of the board of directors (the combination is called *chairperson CEO*).

According to a company statute, employees' representatives can be included in the board of directors (no more than one-third of the board) depending on the number of employees and directors.

2.6.1 Case Study: Renault

The multinational car manufacturer *Renault SA* was founded in Paris by three brothers, Louis Renault, Marcel Renault and Fernand Renault in 1989. Soon it became one of the largest car manufacturers at the national level, as Renault was forced to produce vehicles for the Nazi party, during World War II.

Therefore, after the death of Louis Renault (accused of collaboration with the Nazi party) and the end of World War II, the ownership of the French car manufacturer was transferred to the French government that renamed it as *Régie nationale des usines Renault*. In 1996, the state-owned company was privatised and renamed as *Renault SA*. In the following years, Renault SA commenced a partnership with other car manufacturers, such as Volvo, Nissan, Dacia and Mitsubishi becoming the world's third-largest automotive group (after Volkswagen AG and Toyota Corporation).

Renault SA is listed at the Euronext Paris and its ownership structures, at December 30, 2020, was composed of French State (15.1%), Public (61.88%), Treasure stock (1.53%), Nissan (15%), Daimer (3.10%) and Employees (3.48%).[14]

The CG system of Renault is made of a Board of Directors, Management Committee and Executive committee. The board of directors is made of 17 members (12 appointed by the annual shareholders' general meeting, 1 by the French State and 2 by employees), of which 12 are independent directors.

In order to support the board of directors with its duties, there are three committees, whose members are selected by the board of directors:

- the *Audit and Risk committee*
- the *Governance and compensation committee*
- the *Strategy and Corporate Social Responsibility committee*

Renault SA represents the perfect example of French corporation, where the influence of the state on the corporate decision-making process is still present even though the majority of the ownership belongs to private investors as happens in all public companies worldwide.

2.7 The United Kingdom: The *One-Tier* System

In the nineteenth century, two important corporate law measures were introduced in Britain: The *Joint Stock Company Act,* issued in 1844, and The *Limited Liability Act* issued in 1855.

The former defined stock companies as 'partnerships having a share capital transferable without the express consent of all the partners, certain assurance companies, and partnerships of more than twenty-five membes' (Rix, 1945: 244). Therefore, the legal status with its own legal personality was granted to enterprises with more than twenty-five registered at the *Registrar of companies*, the *Company House*.[15] Companies registered were obliged to file their statutes and annual reports in order to be transparent. The latter (The *Limited Liability Act*) limited the liability of shareholders to the amount of the capital invested, especially if their company declared bankruptcy. Consequently, the number of stock companies and limited liability companies steadily increased in the nineteenth century. In 1914, there were about 65,000 registered companies, the number grew to 200,000 in 1945. In 2012, more than 2.5 million companies were registered and, at the end of March 2020, the number of companies registered reached 4,350,913 including 286,850 in the course of dissolution and liquidation.

In the twentieth century, the CG debate really took off when *Berle and Means* highlighted the consequences of the separation between corporate ownership and management. Their thesis was based on the assumption according to which the separation of ownership from management would have resulted in the inability of shareholders to exercise any form of effective control over the boards of directors elected by them to represent their interests. Berle and Means were also concerned about the growing power held by big corporations, a power that could potentially challenge that of the state one day and, therefore, it needed to be controlled especially with the company's ownership increasingly fragmented, therefore, shareholders had less power to control the management. On the other hand, although shareholders had no difficulty in selling their stakes in case they lost faith in the way the company was run, the failure of the majority of shareholders to make boards of directors accountable to them has firmly placed the agency's problem on the governance agenda.

Therefore, in Anglo-Saxon capitalism system, the traditional fragmentation of the shareholding structure has resulted in the absence of controlling shareholders able to significantly affect governance decisions, among which, the appointment of the members of the board of directors. More specifically, the board of directors often become an expression of the company's top management and its decisions are mainly aimed at maximising the interest of managers rather than that of shareholders.

Companies access the stock exchange to find the financial resources necessary to feed corporate growth in the medium to long term, while investors endeavour to allocate their savings in order to maximise their value. However, considering the high capitalisation achieved, the large number of listed companies, the growing activism on the part of shareholders and the reduced shareholder concentration, a significant culture of CG has developed in the United Kingdom. Consequently, a cornerstone regulation on CG (The Committee on the Financial Aspects of Corporate Governance or simply the Code)[16] for listed companies was published in 1992 by the Cadbury Committee chaired by Adrian Cadbury. The committee defined CG as 'the system by which companies are directed and controlled. Boards of directors are responsible for the governance of their companies. The shareholders' role in governance is to appoint the directors and the auditors and to satisfy themselves that an appropriate governance structure is in place' (Cadbury, 1992: 14). The Code has been revised throughout the years (Greenbury report in 1995; Hampel report in 1998; Turnbull report in 1999; Myners report in 2001; Higgs Report in 2003; Smith report in 2003) in order to consider the growing demands on the UK's CG framework. However, the 'principle of collective responsibility within a unitary board has been a success and – alongside the stewardship activities of investors – played a vital role in delivering high standards of governance and encouraging long-term investment. This remains true today, but the environment in which companies, their shareholders and wider stakeholders operate continues to develop rapidly' (Financial Reporting Council, 2018: 1).

The regulation included in the Code led to an increase in management committees (board committees) with greater powers to non-executive directors (external to the company). These committees, as alternatives to the supervisory board, have the task of monitoring corporate performance in various sectors, such as finance, auditing/budget control, public relations and new technologies.

The innovative point is the role assumed by non-executive directors who, appointed on the basis of their professional skills, have the dual task of supporting operational directors (effectively contributing to 'create added value' within the individual management committees) and to monitor performance of management on the basis of corporate objectives. The presence of a unitary board supported by executive directors who manage the company operations and control it through non-executive directors (external to the company) who operate in specific board committees due to their experience and knowledge. These elements represent the heart of the *one-tier* CG model adopted in the United Kingdom and many other countries as well, such as the United States, Australia, Mexico, India, Sweden, Spain and Turkey.

Besides the Corporate Governance Code, British companies have to follow the *Company Act (2006)* which amended almost entirely the *Companies Act* issued in 1985. Among its peculiarities, the Company Act introduces new provisions for both private and public company and transposes two Directives issued by the European Union (Takeover and Transparency).

2.7.1 Case Study: British Airways

In the United Kingdom, British Airways (BA) represents the flag carrier airline founded in 1974 and headquartered in London. In 2011, BA merged with the Spanish flag carrier airline *Iberia* into Anglo-Spanish multinational airline holding company International Consolidated Airlines Group (IAG) which is comprised of five airline brands (British Airways, Iberia, Vueling, Level and Aer Lingue).

Originally, BA was a state-owned company for thirteen years, however, in 1987 as a part of the privatisation process included in the plan of Thatcher's conservative government.

Regarding the CG model, BA adopts the one-tier system of a unitary board of directors responsible for the management of the company's activities and the development of its strategies. From the annual report issued in 2020, within BA's board of directors, there are two executive directors, CEO and Chief Financial Officer, and five external non-executive directors who scrutinise the board's decisions.[17] The Chairman is responsible for leading the board and ensuring that the directors have equal information. The Board delegates specified duties to specific committees of non-executive directors who have specific skills and knowledge allowing the board to fully fulfil its responsibilities. There are three distinct board committees:

- *nominations committee,* which is responsible for assessing the members of the board, in particular, their knowledge and skills in order to facilitate the selection of candidates and the appointment of candidates of directors by the board;
- *remuneration committee,* which is responsible for reviewing the remuneration policy applied to directors and report recommendations to the board;
- *safety environment and corporate responsibility committee,* which is responsible for informing the board of any safety-related matters.

At IAG level, there is also the *management committee* and the *audit and compliance committee.* The former reviews BA's business and financial plans and reports to the BA's board, which is responsible for reviewing and implementing the committee's recommendations. The latter is entitled to review the activity carried out by the external auditor, the company's accounts and the correct application of the accounting principles and the Corporate Social Responsibility policy implemented.

Notes

1 A firm in which decisions as to current production and distribution and allocation of resources for future production and distribution are made by salaried managers with little or no equity in the firms they operate (Chandler, 1992: 11).
2 Corporate governance codes are sets of business best practices (Akkermans et al., 2007).
3 The active participation of workers aims at preventing managers from only pursuing stakeholders' interests.
4 Those countries are moving from a centrally planned economy to, even if only partial, a market privatised economy.
5 'The term trust refers to the legal relationships created – *inter vivos* or on death – by a person, the settlor, when assets have been placed under the

control of a trustee for the benefit of a beneficiary or for a specified purpose' (Art. 2 Hague Conference on Private International Law – HCCH).
6 The Sherman Antitrust Act (1890), the Federal Trade Commission Act
(1914) and the Clayton Antitrust Act. (1914).
7 https://corporate.ford.com/content/dam/corporate/us/en-us/documents/
governance-and-policies/company-governance-corporate-governance-princi-
ples.pdf
8 'A direct cross holding is defined as a share of one company in another
company. The latter company also the share in the first one' (Adams,
1999: 80).
9 'In a pyramid of two companies, a controlling-minority shareholder holds
a controlling stake in a holding company that, in turn, holds a controlling
stake in an operating company. In a three-tier pyramid, the primary
holding company controls a second-tier holding company that in turn
controls the operating company' (Bebchuk et al., 2000: 449).
10 In case of two types of shares are issued, one for the general public which
has usually no voting rights therefore no voting power. The second type,
issued for founders, executives and family, allows, through the voting
power, the control of the company.
11 *Keiretsu* replaced the *zaibatsu,* which was the typical corporate structure
leading to the success of the Japanese economy until the end of the World
War II. This structure included a family owned holding company and a
bank that financed all the industrial subsidiaries.
12 https://www2.tse.or.jp/tseHpFront/JJK020030Action.do;jsessionid=00BF660B-
2CE2DA4EE45AACB64EF1ACA23
13 An initial public offering (IPO) can be defined as the process of offering
shares of a private corporation to the public in a new stock issuance.
However, private corporations willing to go public and obtain capital by
offering their shares must meet the requirements imposed by the Stock
Markets where the companies want to be listed. In France, the Euronext
Paris is the main stock market that belongs to the Euronext Group.
14 https://www.renaultgroup.com/wp-content/uploads/2020/06/renault-annual_
report-2019_2020.pdf
15 https://www.gov.uk/government/organisations/companies-house
16 https://www.frc.org.uk/getattachment/9c19ea6f-bcc7-434c-b481-f2e29c1c271
a/The-Financial-Aspects-of-Corporate-Governance-(the-Cadbury-Code).pdf
17 https://www.iairgroup.com/~/media/Files/I/IAG/annual-reports/ba/en/british-
airways-plc-annual-report-and-accounts-2020.pdf

Refrences

Adams, M. (1999). Cross holdings in Germany. *Journal of Institutional and
Theoretical Economics (JITE)/Zeitschrift für die gesamte Staatswissenschaft,
155*(1), 80–109.
Airoldi, G., & Zattoni, A. (2006). La coerenza tra strategia, proprietà e gov-
ernance. In A. Zattoni (Ed.), *Assetti proprietari e corporate governance.*
Milano: Egea.
Akkermans, D., Van Ees, H., Hermes, N., Hooghiemstra, R., Van der Laan,
G., Postma, T., & Van Witteloostuijn, A. (2007). Corporate governance in

the Netherlands: An overview of the application of the Tabaksblat Code in 2004. *Corporate Governance: An International Review*, *15*(6), 1106–1118. doi:10.1111/j.1467-8683.2007.00634.

Bebchuk, L. A., Kraakman, R., & Triantis, G. (2000). Stock pyramids, cross-ownership, and dual class equity: the mechanisms and agency costs of separating control from cash-flow rights. In Randall k. Morck (Ed.), *Concentrated corporate ownership* (pp. 295–318). London: University of Chicago Press.

Cadbury, A. (1992). *The financial aspects of corporate governance (Cadbury Report)*. London, UK: The Committee on the Financial Aspect of Corporate Governance (The Cadbury Committee) and Gee and Co, Ltd.

Chandler, A. D. (1962). *Strategy and Structure: Chapters in the History of the Industrial Empire*. Cambridge, MA: M.I.T. Press.

Chandler, A. D. (1977). *The visible hand*. Cambridge, MA: Harvard University Press.

Chandler, A. D. (1992). Managerial enterprise and competitive capabilities. *Business History*, *34*(1), 11–41. doi:10.1080/00076799200000002.

Coase, R. H. (1937). The nature of the firm. *Economica*, *4*(16), 386–405.

Financial Reporting Council. (2018). *The UK Corporate Governance Code*. Retrieved from https://www.icaew.com/technical/corporate-governance/codes-and-reports/uk-corporate-governance-code

Grossman, S. J., & Hart, O. D. (1986). The costs and benefits of ownership: A theory of vertical and lateral integration. *Journal of Political Economy*, *94*(4), 691–719. doi:10.2307/1833199.

Hansmann, H. (1988). Ownership of the firm. *Journal of Law, Economics, & Organization*, *4*(2), 267–304.

Hansmann, H. (1996). *Ownership of enterprise*. Cambridge MA: Harvard University Press.

Kanaya, M. A., & Woo, M. D. (2000). *The Japanese banking crisis of the 1990's: Sources and lessons*. Washington, DC: International Monetary Fund.

Millet-Reyes, B., & Zhao, R. (2010). A comparison between one-tier and two-tier board structures in France. *Journal of International Financial Management & Accounting*, *21*(3), 279–310. doi:10.1111/j.1467-646X.2010.01042.

OECD. (2021). *OECD corporate governance factbook 2021*. Retrieved from https://www.oecd.org/daf/ca/corporate-governance-factbook.pdf.

Porta, R. L., Lopez-de-Silanes, F., Shleifer, A., & Vishny, R. W. (1998). Law and finance. *Journal of Political Economy*, *106*(6), 1113–1155. doi:10.1086/250042.

Porta, R. L., Lopez-de-Silanes, F., Shleifer, A., & Vishny, R. W. (1999). Corporate ownership around the world. *The Journal of Finance*, *54*(2), 471–517. doi:10.1111/0022-1082.00115.

Rix, M. S. (1945). Company law: 1844 and to-day. *The Economic Journal*, *55*(218/219), 242–260.

Sarkar, P., & Singh, A. (2010). Law, finance and development: further analyses of longitudinal data. *Cambridge Journal of Economics*, *34*(2), 325–346.

Williamson, O. E. (1975). *Markets and Hierarchies: Analysis and Antitrust Implications.* New York: Free Press.

Williamson, O. E. (1981). The modern corporation: Origins, evolution, attributes. *Journal of Economic Literature, 19*(4), 1537–1568. doi:10.2307/2 724566.

Zattoni, A. (2011). Who should control a corporation? Toward a contingency stakeholder model for allocating ownership rights. *Journal of Business Ethics, 103*(2), 255–274. doi:10.1007/sl0551-011-0864-3.

3   Corporate Governance in Italy

3.1 The Structural Peculiarities of the Italian Capitalistic System

The structure of the Italian industrial system has changed over the past fifty years due to three fundamental changes. Firstly, the privatisation wave occurred in Italy in the 1980s, one of the most intense in Europe, which made the typical model of state-owned companies vanish, particularly in strategic sectors such as telecommunication, the iron and steel industry and infrastructure. Secondly, the colossal downsizing process that violently hit large business groups that had flourished in the 1900s and that either shut down or were purchased by international investors. Thirdly, the ownership structure of companies has not evolved towards a dispersed shareholding Anglo-Saxon model, in fact, the Italian model is still anchored to a model played by *blockholders* (individuals or families) that own usually more than 50% of the shareholding that impinges on the entry of outside shareholders.

In the 1980s, the Italian industrial system was trying to emerge from the difficult conditions that had definitely destroyed the prosperity in terms of consumption, investments and productivity during the Italian economic miracle of the fifties and sixties (Zamagni, 2012). In addition, one of the greatest difficulties faced by organisations in that period was obtaining financing, due to a weak banking system that could only grant short-term loans to firms, whilst long-term loans were mainly granted to safe state-owned organisations. In addition, the number of listed joint stock companies was extremely low in the 1980s (only 183 companies were listed at the Italian Stock Exchange, compared to thousands of American counterparts) due to the private investor's tendency to invest in bonds and government securities, or more simply in bank deposits. However, the expansion phase of the international business cycle, political stability and a restrictive

DOI: 10.4324/9781003225805-3

monetary policy, which reduced the inflation rate, allowed the main business group to generate cash flow and reduce their debts. Finally, the investment funds launched in the 1980s allowed the stock market to grow, however not as much as they did in Anglo-Saxon countries.

At the beginning of the 1990s, one of the most powerful privatisation processes took place; however, it necessitated a structured reform program in order to provide a legislative framework for regulating managers' and controlling shareholders' behaviour. In addition, it also regulated the functioning of the financial markets due to the presence of international investors who were willing to invest in newly privatised big corporations.

The Italian reform process on CG is based on the Law No.366 issued by the Italian Parliament in 2001 (henceforth 'the 2001 law') through which the government was delegated to issue some legislative decrees regarding new regulations of companies, cooperatives, financial and banking systems; and crimes related to business organisations. The 2001 law was based on what the Mirone Commission[1] (Prodi government) tried to accomplish. More specifically, the commission had to extend the Consolidate Act on Financial Intermediation also known as 'Draghi Law'[2] (Testo Unico delle disposizioni in materia di Intermediazione Finanziaria or TUIF) issued in 1998, which introduced new rules only applicable to the listed companies. Among these rules, the Draghi Law highlighted the necessary transparency of the directors exercising auditing function, and it also introduced a severe punishment for inside traders or any others who did not comply with the requirements imposed by the TUIF. Also in 1998, the Italian Stock Exchange (Borsa Italiana Spa)[3] issued a Corporate Governance Code of Best Practice (The Preda's Code), which started to introduce rules regarding the composition of the board and the internal committees and the impossibility for one person to be appointed to the position of both president of the company and as its CEO, which historically often occurred to Italian corporations.

The Mirone Commission defined several principles of the reform, which were included in the 2001 law through which the government issued four Legislative Decrees in order to implement the principles included in the 2001 Law:

1   Legislative Decree number 61 issued in 2002, related to the introduction of new regulations on company law crimes such as forgery of financial statements;
2   Legislative Decree number 5 issued in 2003, issued in order to resolve disputes on company law cases more efficiently;

3   Legislative Decree number 6 issued in 2003, which is the most important part of the company law reform as it introduced the *one-tier* and *two-tier* CG models in addition to the traditional model. Most importantly, it also introduced the opportunity for both listed and non-listed companies to choose from the three options available;

4   Legislative Decree number 37 issued in 2004, which introduced several amendments to listed companies' legislation.

As a result of this new legal framework, the number of companies listed in the stock market increased, but not as significantly as it did in other countries such as the United States or the United Kingdom. In fact, in the Italian Stock Market, there were only 213 listed companies in 1996, which grew to 257 in 2005,[4] and has since decreased to 227 in 2020 (OECD 2021). The ownership of the companies, particularly non-listed companies, was, and is still today, in the hands of very few shareholders playing the role of *blockholders* (families, individuals and the state). In listed companies, the use of the pyramid groups is characterised by 'a holding company at the top and various layers of subsidiaries below and the entrepreneur typically has the majority of voting rights in every company, either directly in the holding or in-directly in the subsidiaries' (Bianco & Nicodano, 2006: 938). Minority shareholders, on the other hand, are not able to impact the decision-making process, which is entirely influenced by controlling share-holders – i.e. 69 % of Italian companies have up to the three largest shareholders owning more than 50% of the total shareholding. However, 'companies belonging to an integrated group which are controlled by another listed company must have a board with a ma-jority of independent directors as a listing requirement (For the pur-pose of such provisions independent directors cannot serve in the parent company's board)' (OECD 2021: 190). Therefore, at the be-ginning of the new millennium, up to the present day, the public company model was still far away from the full acceptance in the Italian economic system.

Based on this context, we can identify five drivers that led the Italian company law reform:

1   *Applicability*: The reform introduced the possibility of choosing among three different governance models: traditional, one-tier and two-tier models. From a corporate point of view, this deserves credit as the CG reform was meant to be applied to different corporate structures, from small- and medium-sized family-owned

companies for which the one-tier system appears particularly valid, through to large public companies for which either the two-tier system or the traditional model appears adequate. However, even though the possibilities to choose have been made possible, the adoption rate of the two alternative CG models (one- and two-tier systems) is still less than 1% (according to the CONSOB[5] only four listed companies applied the alternative models of CG at the end of 2020).[6] This analysis leads to the conclusion that resistance to change is stronger than the efficiency of the model with respect to the corporate structure and culture.

2   *Efficiency and effectiveness:* It is an undoubted merit of the corporate law reform to have finally clarify the roles and responsibilities among those who carry out audit, management and supervisory functions. However, professionals currently still have to adapt to the new roles and the methodologies to allow for the full application of the new regulations, which is often costlier than it was prior to reform.

3   *Sustainability:* The value creation process is entirely driven by controlling shareholders, while the benefit of creating value for other stakeholders is only indirect and subordinated to the behaviour of the majority shareholders and the organisational behaviour of the management. This is due to the fact that the involvement of minority shareholders or stakeholders in the value creation process is limited in Italy, while in other countries, it is much higher. In addition, while endeavouring to maximise shareholder value, companies should also take into consideration the impact of their activities on society and the environment, which does not rely on the CG model selected. It should be noted that a 'socially responsible' behaviour of the company represents an element of value creation, both of which are recognised and appreciated by the market.

4   *Subsidiarity:* The development and complexity of decision-making process are often linked to the size of the company and the governance models adopted. However, the right level of delegation for the decisions made, who controls processes, how much separation must exist between the Board of Directors and the management and what principles of conduct must be adopted within the organisation, all stem from the choices of shareholders in regard to governance models and managerial behaviours. Overall, the principle subsidiarity is well recognised, in both public and private sectors, as a fundamental principle of 'good governance'. At an organisational level, the principle of subsidiarity

should guide the decision-making processes based on values and skills rather than hierarchical positions, which are considered the main drivers within the different CG models.

On the basis of the aforementioned principles, we can observe that the opportunities offered by the reform of company law to bring the legal structure closer to the entrepreneurial structure has not been optimised up to now. This is due to new CG models still being exclusively guided by the decisions of the majority shareholders. Therefore, researchers and professionals should direct these models towards advanced forms of value creation, demonstrating the importance of long-term value creation and demonstrating that the real value created by a company stems from the value of its intangible 'assets'. Regardless of the type of the CG structure, people should comply with the law and rules of conduct, while corporate control bodies have to verify the compliance with the rules and strategic guidelines in a consistent, professional and transparent manner especially towards the market.

The company law reform entailed the complete revision of the rules relating to the governance of joint stock companies, also granting maximum autonomy to the statutory provisions and protection to all stakeholders. In terms of CG structures, companies can choose from three different models: the ordinary or traditional model; the *one-tier* or dualistic model; the *two-tier* of the monistic model. As the *two-tier* and *one-tier* models are optional, the general rule, sanctioned by art. 2380 of the Italian Civil Code, in fact establishes that the administration and the control of the company, unless the statute provides otherwise, are governed by rules that recall the traditional model.

3.2 The *Traditional* Model of CG

The so-called ordinary or traditional CG model is based on an administrative body (Board of directors or CEO) and on a control body (Board of Statutory Auditors or *collegio sindacale*) representing the shareholders' voice. Members of both bodies are appointed by the general shareholders' meeting which mandatorily appoints an external auditor (auditor or accounting firm) in case of listed companies that are responsible for the audit function (Figure 3.1).

According to the article No. 2380 of the Italian Civil Code, the administrative body of the company is exclusively responsible for the management of the company; therefore, directors should not submissively obey shareholders, but should critically assess their requests with the diligence required by the role they have within the company.

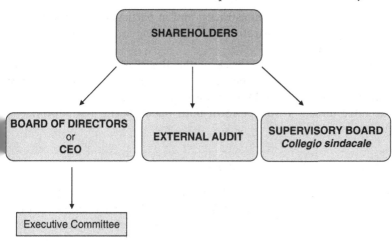

Figure 3.1 The *traditional* corporate governance system.

The number of directors is established in the articles of association, which establish either the minimum or maximum number of directors, while any additional directors have to be appointed by shareholders in the general meeting. Overall, the direction of the company can be appointed to either a board of directors (collegial body) or a single director (CEO). In the case of a collegial body (the board of directors), its powers can be delegated to an Executive Committee or to one or more Executive Directors if the articles of association or the share-holders' meeting allows it (Article 2381 of the Italian Civil Code). In this case, amongst the powers given to the Board of Directors, it carries out a monitoring function over the management activities, in particular, the implementation of the company's strategies and plans.

The Board of Statutory Auditors is responsible for monitoring and controlling the company's account. However, listed companies are obliged to entrust the audit function to either an individual registered auditor or an audit company, registered in the Register kept at the Ministry of Justice and subject to the control performed by the CONSOB. The reform has extended this regulation also to non-listed joint stock companies. However, the articles of association can entrust the audit function to its internal board of statutory auditors on the condition that all members of the board are registered auditors. The Board of Statutory Auditors carries out a legality check action, in fact, pursuant to art. 2403 of the Italian Civil Code, oversees compliance with the law and the Articles of Association, compliance with the principles of proper administration and in particular the adequacy of organisational, administrative and accounting structure adopted and its correct functioning.

Overall, despite the presence of the Board of Statutory Auditors (*collegio sindacale*), *the traditional system* is very similar to the *one-tier* system as the Board of Directors is comprised of executive and non-executive directors who perform both management and supervisory functions.

3.3 The *One-Tier* Model of CG

The *one-tier* or monistic CG system (stemming from the Anglo-Saxon model) is one of the options introduced by the Italian civil code (art. 2409-sexiesdecies) and provides for an administration function exercised by the Board of Directors. Under this model, the control function is appointed to an audit committee (*comitato per il controllo sulla gestione*), which is composed of non-executive directors of the board and replaces the board of statutory auditors (2409-*ocitiesdecies*). Both the members of the board and the audit committees are appointed by the shareholders within the general meetings. However, the members of the audit committee (non-executive directors) are not external subjects like in the traditional and *two-tier* model. This CG structure has developed in Anglo-Saxon countries within public companies, with dispersed shareholding structures. The internal control committee allows to compensate for the lack of direct control exercised by shareholders, therefore monitoring the activities carried out by executive directors. The accounting controls are performed, even in the monistic system, by an external either registered audit company or individual registered auditors. The audit committee monitors the internal control system and the activity of the external auditors. The presence of external auditors stems from the fact the shareholders appoint the Board of Directors (supervised body) whom appoint its controller (audit committee). Therefore, members of the latter must be independent from the board and high professionals.

Overall, the *one-tier* model seems to be simpler and more flexible than the traditional model. However, it also includes some peculiarities and challenges such as the difficulty of entrusting the administration of the company to a sole administrator; the elimination of the board of statutory auditors which is replaced by the control committee appointed by the board of directors; the presence of a single body consisting of a board of directors and a committee established within it, respectively, competent for both the management of the company and the control over it; the accounting control is entrusted to external professionals (with no exception); the board of directors appoints and determines the number of members of the management board (unless the articles of association establishes differently).

In regard to the audit committee, its members are responsible for electing the president of the committee by an absolute majority of its members; monitoring the adequacy of the company's management, organisational structure, the internal control system and performing further tasks appointed by the board of directors. In public companies, which are characterised by a dispersed shareholding, it should be noted that there is a high risk associated with the application of the one-tier system due to the potential conflict of activities between the board of directors and the control committee to the detriment of minority shareholders and corporate creditors. In Italy, this model has not been extensively applied due to the presence of a high concentration of controlling shareholders in corporations mainly individually and family owned.

3.4 The *Two-Tier* Model of CG

The *two-tier* or dualistic model (regulated by art. 2409-*octies* of the Italian civil code) provides for the presence of a management board and a supervisory board. The management of the company is the sole responsibility of the management board, which is made up of at least two members, including non-shareholders, and is appointed by the supervisory board. In the one-tier model, shareholders appoint the controllers (supervisory board), while the supervisory board appoints the management board whose members exercise similar functions of executive directors in both traditional and one-tier systems. The regulation of the board of directors in the traditional system can be applied to the members of the management board (art. 2409-*undecies*), while the rules applied to the board of statutory auditors can be applied to the members of the supervisory board (art. 2409-*quaterdecies*).

The main difference between the traditional system and the two-tier system lies in the fact that in the traditional system shareholders appoint both the board of directors (*Consiglio di amministrazione*) and the controlling body (board of statutory auditors – *Collegio sindacale*), while in the two-tier system, the shareholders appoint the controlling body (supervisory board) that, in turn, appoints the management board. Moreover, in the traditional system, shareholders approve the financial statements, while in the two-tier system, the financial statements are approved by the supervisory board and shareholders have to appoint an external registered auditor (individual or audit company). However, in the traditional system if the company is not listed in the stock market, 'the article of association can reserve the audit of the accounts to the board of statutory registered auditors' (Ferrarini, Giudici, & Richter, 2005: 676).

Even though the two-tier model is applied in both Germany and Italy, there is a difference between the German and the Italian version. In the former, members of the management board (Vorstand) are only composed of executive directors, while in the Italian counterpart, non-executive directors are also present within the board. In addition, workers' representatives do not have a place in the Italian board of directors like in Germany (*co-determination*). In addition, the German two-tier model, the supervisory board (*Aufsichtsrat*), not only plays a supervisory role over the management board (*Vorstand*) but also exercises a function of strategic management. Unfortunately, the interdependence of the supervisory board members from the management board does not exclude the risk of collusion between these two bodies, as happened in Germany in the Volkswagen case in 2008 (*Dieselgate*).[7]

3.4.1 Case Study: Intesa San Paolo S.p.A.

The adoption, by listed joint-stock companies, of the *two-tier* CG model in the Italian territory is mainly chosen by banks, among which, Intesa San Paolo S.p.A. represents one the leading banking groups with 4700 branches and 13.5 million customers, operating in different markets, including Central-Eastern Europe, Middle East and North Africa.

Intesa San Paolo S.p.A. was the result of an important merge of two large Italian banks: Banca Intesa and Sanpaolo IMI in 2007. As of June 2021, the share capital was equal to €10,084,445,147.92, divided into 19,430,463,305 shares. Among the main shareholders, there is Compagnia di San Paolo (6.119%), BlackRock Inc. (5.005%) and Fondazione Cariplo (3.948%), while 84.928% of the share capital is available on the stock market to share.

Intesa San Paolo S.p.A. carries out its activities through the following business units:

- the *Bank of Territories* (La banca dei Territori): this division is responsible for strengthening its relations with individual customers, small- and medium-sized enterprises and non-profit entities; through a widespread presence in the territory;
- the *Corporate and Investment Banking Division*: this division aims

at developing global partnerships through supporting cross-border activities of its customers in 29 countries;

• the *Foreign Banking Division:* this division controls the commercial banking activities in non-European countries such as Albania, Bosnia-Herzegovina, Croatia, Egypt, Russian Federation, Czech Republic, Romania, Serbia, Slovakia, Slovenia and Hungary;

• the *Private Banking Division:* this division aims at meeting the needs of private customers through the offering of specific products and services tailored to *High Net Worth Individuals*;

• the *Asset Management Division:* this division aims at providing asset management solutions;

• the *Insurance Division*: this division offers insurance and products for pensioners;

• the *Capital Light Bank*: this division focuses on non-performing loans and non-strategic equity investments.

Regarding the CG model, Intesa San Paolo S.p.A. is one of the few listed stock joint companies that decided to adopt the *two-tier* model, which provides for the presence of a Supervisory Board (*Consiglio di Sorveglianza*) and a Management board (*Consiglio di gestione*). The nuance of the Italian version of the two-tier model is that members of both the Supervisory Board and Management board are appointed by the Shareholders, whilst in the German model, the supervisory board appoints the members of the management board.

The Supervisory Board, composed of 15 up to 21 members, carries out its activities through several committees: *Internal Control Committee, Appointments Committee , Remuneration Committee, Risks Committee and Committee for transactions with related parties of Intesa Sanpaolo S.p.A.*

The Management Board appoints a managing director, on the recommendation of the Supervisory Board, from the members of the management board, and it represents the only director with full decisional power among which: overseeing company management and the execution of the resolutions of the Management Board; being in charge with the management of personnel; determining the operational directives; reporting to the Management Board regarding the general trend of management and its foreseeable evolution. The chairman of the Management Board, as a legal representative of the company, has the functions of driving and coordinating the activities of the Management Board, ensuring a collaborative relationship with the supervisory board; however, it does not hold an executive power which is given to the managing director. Being a listed company, Intesa San

Paolo S.p.A. has to appoint a registered auditing company (KPMG S.p.A.), which is responsible for verifying the regularity and accuracy of its financial statements.

However, the application of the two-tier model can be considered as a failure due to its inability to adapt to changes quickly. In fact, in May 2013, the company did not have a proper management board as the majority of members did not have the necessary skills to carry out their activities. Consequently, an extraordinary general shareholders' meeting was summoned on 14 December 2014 to decide whether to keep the dualistic CG model. Even though Intesa San Paolo S.p.A endeavoured to keep the dualistic model at the extraordinary shareholders' meeting held on 26 February 2016, Intesa Sanpaolo decided to apply the one-tier CG model in order to ensure an efficient management and effective control activities through the presence of a Board of Directors and an internal Management Control Committee, both appointed by shareholders.

3.5 The Italian Corporate Governance Code of Best Practice (Preda's code)

Throughout the years, corporations have made CG choices in order to fully meet stakeholders' expectations. Consequently, CG has become one of the most effective drivers of the value creation processes of companies.

Business organisations operate within a legal framework, which comprises a binding and a voluntary part. The former is represented by a collection of norms regulating the structure and the functioning of companies under a legal point of view. In Italy, the legal source of corporation (hard law) is the Civil Code (considering all its amendments introduced through the Company Law reform operated in 2004) and the Consolidate Act on Financial Intermediation or TUIF (Testo Unico delle disposizioni in materia di Intermediazione Finanziaria), introduced through Legislative Decree No. 58/1998). The rationale behind the drafting of the TUIF was to provide general principles and leave technical specifications to regulations and self-regulations of the markets and financial intermediaries. In this regard, self-regulation (soft law) has found space to complete the framework of CG practices. As we will see, this regulatory instrument has characteristics of flexibility and elasticity, which make it suitable, much more than the legislative instrument, to dictate rules capable of adapting to the needs of practice in a simple and rapid way.

Among the self-regulation tools, the Corporate Governance Code of Best Practice (hereafter, the Code) is considered a reference model for the best practice towards which to strive, designed for companies that intend to improve their competitiveness by voluntarily adapting their governance systems to the proposed solutions. These solutions are changed by the statutory and administrative practices of companies that have shown themselves to be more sensitive and attentive to pursuing advanced models of CG and are set as standards at an international level. According to the Global Corporate Governance Forum, 'Corporate governance codes of best practice are sets of nonbinding recommendations aimed at improving and guiding the governance practices of corporations within a country's specific legal environment and business context. These codes are typically based on principles and focus on country-specific issues' (GCGF, 2015: 21). Therefore, taking into consideration the specificities of the various legal systems, and the peculiarities of the individual corporate systems, the editors of the Code drew inspiration from itineraries already covered in some foreign systems.

However, a common principle among all the international Codes available is the voluntary compliance of listed companies with the Code regulations. However, in case of non-compliance with the Code, according to the principle *comply-or-explain*,[8] listed companies are to compulsorily explain the reasons for this choice. The foundation of this principle is 'to allow firms some flexibility – i.e. to choose which CG structure to adopt to better pursue their objectives – while guaranteeing better transparency to the market' (Cuomo, Mallin, & Zattoni, 2016: 223).

Based on the hierarchical relevance of the issuer, three levels of Codes can be identified:

1   Codes issued by international authorities, in order to share and spread worldwide good governance practices and, at the same time, to increase CG standards. Some typical issuers of these codes are the Organization for Economic Co-operation and Development (OECD),[9] the Commonwealth[10] and the International Corporate Governance Network (ICGN).[11]

2   Codes issued internally by the company itself in order to demonstrate the correct application of the governance principles to the stakeholders (i.e. employees, suppliers, investors).

3   Codes issued by institutions, such as the stock exchange in order to positively impact on CG practices at the national level. The rest of this chapter will focus on the Italian Code, giving also account to some other codes adopted in different countries.

The main reason that led different countries to Code draft is the common belief the existence of a CG Code produces a positive effect on the growth of the demand for risk capital, as savers have more faith in the stock market, which in turn influences the destiny of joint-stock companies through the stock trade fluctuations within the stock market. In addition, from an international perspective, the globalisation of companies and markets leads to the adoption of best practice rules that allow the international financial community to equally evaluate the behaviour of companies. Therefore, in each country, CG rules have to be aligned with those in use in other countries. This allows both to make comparisons between the legal systems and to avoid being penalised in the international comparison in terms of competition between systems.

In order to better understand the philosophy behind the Code, we proceed with an analysis of the objectives it aims to achieve, more specifically:

- It is a tool that allows companies to access the capital market and, at the same time, it is capable of guaranteeing a high level of protection for savers and institutional investors by showing the company's seriousness and its commitment to rules. It should be noted the importance of the current role of institutional investors, who until a few years ago, had shown their dissatisfaction with the negative performance of financial instruments issued by companies in which they had invested in. Nowadays, each action taken by listed companies generates an impact on the price of its securities, given the large amount of financial instruments held by these subjects. Therefore, investors tend to defend the value of their investments by monitoring and controlling the activities of managers.
- It shows a corporate organisation model suitable for managing the proper control of business risks and potential conflicts of interest, which can always interfere in relations between directors and shareholders and between controlling and minority shareholders. However, this organisational model ought not to be understood as a rigid set of rules and procedures to be applied without a real commitment to it, but as an opportunity for the development of markets and companies.
- It aims at maximising shareholders' value through the implementation of a good CG system, which in the long term should trigger a virtuous circle in terms of corporate efficiency and integrity capable of having a positive impact on the interests of

stakeholders. However, despite the formal reference to interests other than that of the shareholders, in practice, the Code adopts a notion of efficiency aimed at maximising the interests of the shareholders. Overall, the principles on which the Code should be based on are, respectively, flexibility, organisational freedom and transparency as they allow higher adaptability by companies and more protection for savers and institutional investors.

In regard to the Italian context, the first Corporate Governance Code of Best Practice (hereafter, the Italian Code) was issued by the Italian stock exchange, Borsa Italiana S.p.A[12] in 1999, drafted by the *Corporate Governance Committee,* chaired by Prof. Stefano Preda and made of experts representing different categories of subjects such as issuers, institutional investors, banks, insurance companies and auditors. Since its first version (1999), the Italian Code has been updated and new versions were issued, more specifically in 2002, 2006, 2010 (only in regard to directors' remuneration), 2011, 2014, 2015 and 2018. The latest version of the Italian Code was issued and approved in 2020 and came into force on 1 January 2021.[13]

The Italian Code is addressed to all companies with shares listed on the Electronic Stock Market (*Mercato Telematico Azionario*) managed by Borsa Italiana S.P.A. The compliance with the Code is voluntary and, in case of listed companies refusing to comply with the Code, they have to provide reasons for the refusal (*comply or explain principle*).

The Code is divided into six principles (role of the administrative body; composition of corporate bodies; functioning of the administrative body and the role of its president; appointment of directors and self-evaluation of the administrative body; remuneration system; internal control system and risk management system), twenty principles, which define the objectives of good governance, and thirty-seven related recommendations that indicate the behaviours that the Code considers necessary to adopt in order to achieve the objectives indicated in the principles.

Conversely, listed companies complying with the Code have to draft a publicly available report, which provides accurate information regarding the compliance with the regulations included in the Code and how it has been applied. In addition, companies have to explain partial or different implementation of its rules in the report. When some recommendations do not perfectly align with the hard law, companies do not need to explain why they did not follow that specific recommendations.

The Corporate Governance Committee monitors the application of the Code at the national level and it analyses the best practice at the international level in order to assess the potential development of the national Code in a new updated version. In this regard, the Committee asks questions and clarifications (through a Q&A section) to listed companies that have adopted the Code in order to understand potential weaknesses of the code and transform them into future strengths.

3.6 The International Corporate Governance Codes of Best Practice

The United Kingdom was the first country to issue a Corporate Governance Code of Best Practice (the Code), the *Financial Aspects of Corporate Governance*[14] or Cadbury Report issued in 1992 by the committee chaired by Adrian Cadbury. According to the international review on Corporate Governance Codes conducted by Cuomo et al. (2016), two important international organisations issued their *Principles of Corporate Governance* after the issuance of the Cadbury's Code, more specifically, the Organization for Economic Co-operation and Development (OECD) and the International Corporate Governance Network (ICGN) both in 1999. At the global level, besides the United Kingdom, only eight countries issued the Code (South Africa and Canada in 1994; Australia and France in 1995; Spain in 1996; USA, Japan and The Netherlands in 1997), and this number reached 34 by 2002.

3.6.1 The United Kingdom

One of the main points highlighted in the first code of CG (*Cadbury's report*) was the importance given to non-executive directors in order to establish and maintain high standards of CG through the control function they are called upon to perform. The Code requires a minimum number of non-executive dependent directors who have the right to access to the same type and quality of information as executive directors. In addition, non-executive directors should not stay within the same committee for too long in order to preserve their independence. Cadbury's report recommends that within the *audit, nomination* and *remuneration committees* the majority should be of non-executive directors.

In 1995, the *Greenbury's report* was issued, which did not add major amendments to the Cadbury's report besides some clarifications in regard to directors' remuneration and their annual report submitted to the audit committee. In 1998, a new committee chaired by Ronal Hampel was established, and a new report was issued (*Hampel's report*) through which the *board balance principle* was set to emphasise the necessary equilibrium in the composition of the board of directors. On the basis of the analysis in regard to the degree of implementation of the recommendations of both the Cadbury and Greenbury's code, Hampel drafted the *Combined Code in* 1998, followed by an updated version issued in 2000. It is composed of two parts: *Principles of Corporate Governance* and *Code of Best Practices*. Overall, the Combined Code offers an orderly and systematic presentation of all the instances proposed by the reports that precede it (Cadbury, Greenbury and Hampel). In particular, the *Principles of Corporate Governance* summarize the essence of the British CG experience, while the *Code of Best Practice*, which is structured in a series of articles commenting on each of the Principles, offers a series of provisions that clarify the content of each principle.

In 2003, two important reports were issued, the *Higgs' report*, which was promoted by the Department of Trade and Industry, and the *Smith's report,* which was promoted by the Financial Reporting Council. Both documents often refer to each other and aim to provide useful contributions to a review of the 2000 Combined Code. The former report better specified the role and importance of non-executive directors within the board of directors while the latter, regulating the audit committee, recommends the presence of at least three independent directors. These reviews resulted in the publication of the Combined Code on Corporate Governance, which took place in July 2003, which replaced the old version drawn up by the Hampel Commission in 1998. The revised version of the Combined Code includes all the corrections proposed by the Higgs and Smith reports as well as some suggestions from the 1999 Turnbull Report, which dealt with internal controls. Since 2003, every two years, the Financial Report Council (FRC) published an updated version based on the responses provided to the questions arisen during the consultation period when the FRC asked for the areas of potential improvements to the current version of the Code. Therefore, seven updated versions (2006,[15] 2008,[16] 2010,[17] 2012,[18] 2014,[19] 2016[20] and 2018) of the Combined Code have been published since the first version issued in 2003. In the latest version, issued in 2018[21] effective since January 2019, the Combined Code emphasises the flexibility in the application of the code but, at the same time, the high value given to good CG in order to achieve and maintain long-term sustainable success.

3.6.2 France

We can identify three main sources of soft regulation in France: the Corporate Governance Code for listed companies (*Code de gouvernemet d'entreprise des sociétés cotées*) issued by the AFEP[22] (Association française des entreprises privées) and the MEDEF[23] (Mouvement des entreprises de France); the Recommendations on Corporate Governance (*Recommandations sur legouvernement d'entreprise*) issued by AFG (Association Francaise de la gestion financière); the recommendations issued by the AMF (Autorité des Marchés Financieres).

Although the *code de commerce* (Articles L.225–37-4 and L.225–68), by incorporating the *Loi sur la modernization de economics*[24] (law on modernisation of economics), has decreed the AFEP and MEDEF code as a code of reference, companies have to decide which regulation to comply to within their Corporate Governance Statement (*declaration sur le gouvernement d'entreprise*). France is one of the few countries where the Code is not subjected to public consultation in order to acquire potential ideas of improvements or highlight weaknesses. In addition, France and the United Kingdom are the only two countries drafting a specific CG code for small- and medium-sized companies (*the MiddleNext code*).[25]

Regarding the most accredited Corporate Governance Code for listed companies, the AFEP-MEDEF code, several times, this Code has been modified and updated throughout the years. More specifically:

* in 1995, a first report was issued by the committee chaired by Marc Vienot (*Vienot's report*), which regulated the composition of the board and its tasks. In particular, the report recommended a balance in the number of executive and non-executive directors within the board of directors and the establishment of committees for carrying out specific activities of the board (audit; nomination; remuneration committee);
* in 1999, a second report issued by a committee still chaired by Marc Vienot (*Vienot's report II*) through which the *comply or explain* was introduced. In addition, this report provides further recommendations on compensation system and the functioning of the both the board of directors and its committees;
* in 2002, following the Enron crisis, a third report was drafted by a committee chaired by Daniel Bouton (*Bouton's report*)[26] in order to re-establish investors' confidence. In this regard, the report recommended a higher independence of directors, legal auditors and better provision of financial information;

- in 2003, the Vienot I, II and Bouton's report were transformed and further developed to draft the 'corporate code of listed companies';
- in 2007 and 2008, some recommendations were included in the Code, especially in regard the remuneration of the company's officers;
- in 2010, the main recommendations made and added to the Code regarded the presence of at least 40% of women;
- in 2013, it was introduced a principle according to which shareholders have the right to vote on Directors' compensation (*say on pay principle*).[27] In addition, there was the reinforcement of the *comply or explain* principle and the creation of the *High Committee on Corporate Governance;*
- in 2015, based on the recommendations made by the AMF, the disposal of significant assets was included in the Code;
- in 2016, further recommendations were made in regard to Corporate Social Responsibility, the independence of directors and compensation of non-executive directors;
- in 2018, a major set of recommendations was made, among which the specification of the board of directors' purpose was to pursue long-term value creation by considering the impact of the activities carried out by the company from an environmental and social point of view. In addition, the number of members of the High Committee on Corporate Governance was extended to nine members;
- in 2020, the latest Corporate Governance Code was issued for listed corporations.[28] The new Code, made of 28 recommendations, spread across 41 pages (compared to the first 20-page version), covers two main aspects: women's career paths, and the difference between directors and employees' salary. In regard to the first aspect, the Code recommends an improved equilibrium between male and female members of the board of directors and within the committees. In relation to the second aspect, the Code recommends an explanation within the annual report drafted by the board of directors, regarding the coefficients used to calculate the compensation of the both directors and employees allowing, therefore, an objective comparison.

3.6.3 Germany

The first version of the German Corporate Governance Code (*Deutscher Corporate Governance Kodex*) was drafted by a government commission chaired by Gerhard Cromme, and it was published in 2002. The Cromme commission's Code was based on the report previously drafted by the commission established in 2000 and chaired by Theodor Baums[29] and on the research conducted by private entities. The review of the Code is a regular activity performed by the Commission, which annually revise the Code with the aim of ensuring that the Code is still able to depict best practice CG.

Since its first version issued in 2002,[30] the German Corporate Governance Code (*Deutscher Corporate Governance Kodex*) has been amended and updated twelve times, more specifically in 2003,[31] 2005,[32] 2006,[33] 2007,[34] 2009,[35] 2010,[36] 2012,[37] 2013,[38] 2014,[39] 2015[40] and 2017,[41] while the latest version of the Code was issued in 2019[42] and published in the Federal Gazette 20 March 2020.

In the annual declaration of conformity to the § 161 of the Stock Corporation Act (*Aktiengesetz*), in which the Code has a legal basis, it states that listed companies have to either justify the partial adoption or refuse to adopt the Code. However, the implementation of the Code remains not mandatory and, above all, transparent and flexible in order to allow companies to consider both their specific needs and those of the sector where it operates.

Three distinctive elements were highlighted in the Code (*Kodex*):

1   The purpose of the Code, which is to provide rules for the management and supervision of German companies listed on the stock market and to simultaneously incorporate standards adopted at national and international levels in order to achieve the correct and responsible management of the company. These regulations largely refer to the German Stock Corporation Act (*Aktiengesetz*).

2   A full description of the *two-tier* model of CG, which is composed of a supervisory board (*Aufsichtsrat*) and a management board (*Vorstand*).

3   It is stated that observance of the recommendations contained in the code takes place on a completely voluntary basis, and nevertheless, it is specified that companies are required to communicate the failure to implement some of them, explaining the reasons that led to this decision (*comply or explain*).

One of the key elements emphasised in the *Deutscher Corporate Governance Kodex* is the necessary independence of the members of the supervisory board. In addition, the Code recommends the establishment of committees within the supervisory board, and not in the management board, where independent skilled professionals are able to carry out specific tasks (i.e. audit, personnel, nomination and working committees).

The code is divided (2020 version) into twenty-five principles and sixty-four recommendations and suggestions[43] aiming at supporting the management and the supervision of listed companies in Germany by different subjects such as investors, employees and customers. These principles, which are implemented through the recommendations and suggestions provided in the Code, represent the common standards of good governance recognised at national and international levels.

3.6.4 Japan

According to the *Japan Revitalization Strategy,*[44] revised in 2015 by Cabinet Decision, the Stewardship and Corporate Governance Code, 'the two wheels of a cart',[45] able to drive companies' success increasing corporate value and reaching a sustainable growth in the middle-long term. In this regard, the Tokyo Stock Exchange (TSE) and the Financial Service Agency established a Council[46] of eternal experts such as academics, investors and managers joining together in order to monitor the adoption of the Codes and, above all, improving them through a previous consultation period during which the Council proposes changes and improvements to both Code and the related Guidelines that have to be followed by listed companies in order to correctly apply the Code of Corporate Governance.

The first Corporate Governance Code was issued in Japan in 1995, and since then, several revisions have been made with the latest version published on 11 June 2021.[47] The adoption of the Code, like in any other countries, is not mandatory. However, the refusal to adopt the Code has to be justified in accordance with the principle to *comply or explain.* The Code is based on the compliance with five general principles, each of which is further clarified with sub-principles and supplementary principles (introduced by the word *should*). The main five principles are as follows:

1 *Securing the Rights and Equal Treatment of Shareholders:* especially in regard to minority and foreign shareholders who have to be able to exercise their rights as effectively as controlling shareholders.

2 *Appropriate Cooperation with Stakeholders Other Than Shareholders:* sustainable growth is reached in the long run as long as the board and the management are able to foster

cooperation among all stakeholders (clients, staff, creditors and local communities) involved in the creation of sustainable growth.

3   *Ensuring Appropriate Information Disclosure and Transparency*: in order to establish a productive discussion with the shareholders, companies have to provide them with precise, flawless and appropriate information pertaining both financial results and non-financial matters such as strategies and risks.

4   *Responsibilities of Board*: regardless of the CG model chosen (a company with statutory auditors; a company with three committees; a company with an audit and supervisory committee), the Board of directors has to set an appropriate corporate strategy; favouring a safe risk-taking approach; objectively supervise directors and managers.

5   *Dialogue with Shareholders*: at the basis of a mid-long term sustainable growth all shareholders should be given attention from senior managers and directors, especially in regard to their doubts over the business policies implemented that should be appropriately explained.

In regard to the last Corporate Governance Code (issued in 2021), the *Council of Experts Concerning the Follow-up of Japan's Stewardship Code and Japan's Corporate Governance Code* proposed the following improvements of the current Code such as enhancing board independence; promoting diversity in terms of gender and internationality; increasing attention towards sustainability, under an environmental, social and governance standpoint, in terms of activities carried out and policies implemented.

3.6.5 The United States

In the United States, there are three main sources of corporate law:

1   *State corporate laws* that regulate in each State the establishment of corporations, either privately held or publicly traded; the rights and duties of directors and officers in managing the company; shareholders' rights. In addition, in order to resolve the controversy, each state considers the Model Business Corporation Act which comprised a set of law drafted by the American Bar Association.

2   *Federal security laws*:

- The Security Act 1933, which regulates the share trading activities of both public and private companies;

- The Security Exchange Act 1934, which regulates the disclosure of information for public companies;
- The Public Company Accounting Reform and Investor Protection Act issued in 2002 also known as *Sarbanes-Oxley Act*,[48] which regulates all the facts not specifically regulated by state corporate laws. In particular, the law, made of eleven sections, was drafted as a reaction to the major corporate and accounting scandals such as Enron and WorldCom. The *Sarbanes-Oxley Act* put particular emphasis on the criminal responsibilities of the board of directors in case of misconduct;
- The Dodd-Frank Wall Street Reform and Consumer Protection Act of 2010 also known as *Dodd-Frank Act*,[49] which was drafted following the global financial and economic crisis that occurred in 2007/2008, in order to enhance the financial system by increasing its both accountability and transparency and to defend American citizens against illegal financial activities.
- Regulations issued by the Security and Exchange Commission (SEC)[50] which implements the rules included in both the Sarbanes-Oxley (2002) and Dodd-Frank Act (2010). The SEC also oversees the rules and operations of both the New York Stock Exchange and the Nasdaq Stock Market, which are the two largest stock exchange operators worldwide with a capitalisation of listed companies of 24.4 trillion (NYSE) and 20.87 trillion (Nasdaq) US dollars in 2021.

Listed companies have to abide by the rules included in the Corporate Governance Guidelines issued by NYSE[51] and Nasdaq,[52] requiring the majority of directors to be independent. An additional best practice recommendation issued by the American Law Institute (ALI), also known as the 'Principles of Corporate Governance', considers a director as independent only if he/she does not have any 'significant relationship' with the company or with its senior executives. Therefore, the 'independence' of directors especially within the committees, in particular, the audit committee is an essential prerequisite for the correct function of the board of directors. Last but not least, an important set of 'best practice' is represented by the recommendations delivered by the National Association of Corporate Directors, the Blue Ribbon Commission, the Business Roundtable[53] and CII.[54]

Overall, according to the principles recommended by Nasdaq and NYSE, the board of directors has to fulfil its responsibilities in the most legal and ethical manner, in order to meet both current and evolving challenges faced by organisations.

Notes

1 Antonino Mirone was the president of the Mirone Commission established during the Prodi government I (1996–1998).
2 Mario Draghi was the president of the Draghi Commission and since February 13th, 2021 is the Italian Prime Minister.
3 https://www.borsaitaliana.it/homepage/homepage.htm
4 https://www.consob.it/documents/46180/46181/rel2005.pdf/951ab135-11e7–4668-a8f9-d35bfd0ad7d4
5 CONSOB (Commissione Nazionale per le Società e la Borsa) represents the Italian government commission that regulates the Italian stock market.
6 https://www.consob.it/documents/46180/46181/rcg2020.pdf/023c1d9b-ac8b-49a8-b650-3a4ca2aca53a
7 Volkswagen admitted that in approximately eleven million cars at global level there was a defeat device installed in order to distort the emission testing, causing a serious breach of environmental, criminal, corporate, insurance, civil and consumer law.
8 The *comply-or-explain* principle was introduced by art. 20 of Directive No. 34 issued by the European Union in 2013.
9 https://www.oecd.org/corporate/Corporate-Governance-Factbook.pdf
10 https://old.ecseonline.com/PDF/CACG%20Guidelines%20%20Principles%20for%20Corporate%20Governance%20in%20the%20Commonwealth.pdf
11 http://icgn.flpbks.com/icgn-global-governance-principles-2017/
12 https://www.borsaitaliana.it/homepage/homepage.en.htm
13 https://www.borsaitaliana.it/comitato-corporate-governance/codice/2020.pdf
14 https://www.frc.org.uk/getattachment/9c19ea6f-bcc7–434c-b481-f2e29c1c271a/The-Financial-Aspects-of-Corporate-Governance-(the-Cadbury-Code).pdf
15 https://www.frc.org.uk/getattachment/8238c251-5cfe-43b7-abc0–4318ccbdc0fd/Combined-Code-2006-(Oct-version).pdf
16 https://www.frc.org.uk/getattachment/56920102-feeb-4da7–84f7–1061840af9f0/Combined-Code-Web-Optimized-June-2008.pdf
17 https://www.frc.org.uk/getattachment/31631a7a-bc5c-4e7b-bc3a-972b7f17d5e2/UK-Corp-Gov-Code-June-2010.pdf
18 https://www.frc.org.uk/getattachment/e322c20a-1181-4ac8-a3d3-1fcfbcea7914/UK-Corporate-Governance-Code-(September-2012).pdf
19 https://www.frc.org.uk/getattachment/59a5171d-4163-4fb2–9e9d-daefcd7153b5/UK-Corporate-Governance-Code-2014.pdf
20 https://www.frc.org.uk/getattachment/ca7e94c4-b9a9–49e2-a824-ad76a322873c/UK-Corporate-Governance-Code-April-2016.pdf
21 https://www.frc.org.uk/getattachment/88bd8c45–50ea-4841-95b0-d2f4f48069a2/2018-UK-Corporate-Governance-Code-FINAL.pdf
22 AFEP is an association which representing 111 of the largest private corporations operating in France [https://afep.com/].
23 The MEDEF is the biggest network of SMEs operating in France [https://www.medef.com/].
24 https://www.legifrance.gouv.fr/loda/id/JORFTEXT000019283050/
25 https://www.fsa.go.jp/en/refer/councils/corporategovernance/reference/france-middlenext.pdf
26 http://paris-europlace.net/files/a_09–23-02_rapport-bouton_uk.pdf
27 The *say on pay* principle was modified through the Sapin Law II in 2016

(LOI no 2016-1691) which also introduced the French Anticorruption Agency (*Agence Française Anticorruption* – AFA).

28 https://www.se.com/ww/en/Images/afep-medef-code-revision-january-2 020-en_tcm564–134746.pdf

29 The commission chaired by Theodor Baums was set up by the German government in 2000 with the aim of identifying possible gaps in the German governance and corporate control regulations and advising for a reform of the German Stock Corporation Act (*Aktiengesetz*).

30 https://www.dcgk.de/files/dcgk/usercontent/en/download/code/D_CorGov_ final_2002_11.pdf.

31 https://www.dcgk.de/files/dcgk/usercontent/en/download/code/D_CorGov_ final_2003.pdf

32 https://www.dcgk.de/files/dcgk/usercontent/en/download/code/D_CorGov_ final_2005.pdf

33 https://www.dcgk.de/files/dcgk/usercontent/en/download/code/D_CorGov_ final_2006.pdf

34 https://www.dcgk.de/files/dcgk/usercontent/en/download/code/D_CorGov_ final_2007.pdf

35 https://www.dcgk.de/files/dcgk/usercontent/en/download/code/D_CorGov_ final_2009.pdf

36 https://www.dcgk.de/files/dcgk/usercontent/en/download/code/D_CorGov_ final_2010.pdf

37 https://www.dcgk.de/files/dcgk/usercontent/en/download/code/D_CorGov_ final_2012.pdf

38 https://www.dcgk.de/files/dcgk/usercontent/en/download/code/D_CorGov_ final_2013.pdf

39 https://www.dcgk.de/files/dcgk/usercontent/en/download/code/140624_German_ Corporate_Goverance_Code_EN.pdf

40 https://www.dcgk.de/files/dcgk/usercontent/en/download/code/2015-05-05_ Corporate_Governance_Code_EN.pdf

41 https://www.dcgk.de/files/dcgk/usercontent/en/download/code/170214_Code.pdf

42 https://www.dcgk.de//files/dcgk/usercontent/en/download/code/191216_German_ Corporate_Governance_Code.pdf

43 Suggestions can be easily recognised as they are introduced by the word 'should'.

44 https://japan.kantei.go.jp/kan/topics/sinseichou01_e.pdf

45 https://www.jpx.co.jp/english/equities/listing/cg/tvdivq0000008jdy-att/2015 0807-2.pdf

46 Council of Experts Concerning the Follow-up of Japan's Stewardship Code and Japan's Corporate Governance Code.

47 https://www.jpx.co.jp/english/equities/listing/cg/tvdivq0000008jdy-att/2021 0611.pdf

48 https://www.govinfo.gov/content/pkg/PLAW-107publ204/html/PLAW-1 07publ204.htm

49 https://www.govinfo.gov/content/pkg/PLAW-111publ203/html/PLAW-111 publ203.htm

50 https://www.sec.gov/page/regulation

51 https://www.nyse.com/publicdocs/nyse/listing/NYSE_Corporate_Governance_ Guide.pdf

52 https://ir.nasdaq.com/static-files/3e005938-23c9-4adc-b917-a4e3beca626c

53 https://www.businessroundtable.org/
54 https://www.cii.org/cgadvisorycouncil

References

Bianco, M., & Nicodano, G. (2006). Pyramidal groups and debt. *European Economic Review*, *50*(4), 937–961. doi:10.1016/j.euroecorev.2004.11.001.

Cuomo, F., Mallin, C., & Zattoni, A. (2016). Corporate governance codes: A review and research agenda. *Corporate Governance: An International Review*, *24*(3), 222–241. doi: 10.1111/corg.12148.

Ferrarini, G., Giudici, P., & Richter, M. S. (2005). Company law reform in Italy: Real progress?. *Rabels Zeitschrift für ausländisches und internationales Privatrecht/The Rabel Journal of Comparative and International Private Law*, *69*(H. 4), 658–697.

GCGF. (2015). Developing corporate governance code of best practice. *International Bank for Reconstruction and Development/ The World Bank* (1–91), vol. 1. Washington DC.

OECD. (2021). Studi economici dell'OCSE: Italia 2021. OECD Publishing, Paris. https://doi.org/10.1787/85d51ef5-it.

Zamagni, V. (2012). The Italian 'Economic Miracle' revisited: New markets and American technology. In *Great Britain, France, Germany and Italy and the Origins of the EEC, 1952–1957* (pp. 197–226). De Gruyter. doi:10.1515/9783110874365.197

4 What Is the Most Suitable Corporate Governance Model?

4.1 The Evolution of CG

The challenges that companies have faced throughout the years have inevitably changed the functioning mechanisms of companies and, above all, the manner to respond to these crises. In particular, the financial and economic crisis that hit the globe in 2007/2008 and the current pandemic, as a consequence of the powerful and restless outbreak of the coronavirus disease (COVID-19), have had strong repercussions on all national economic systems unfortunately leading many business organisations to shut down although the efforts made by national governments in order to financially support companies and, at the same, avoid massive layoffs and the rise of the unemployment rate.

Corporate governance, defined by Sir Adrian Cadbury in 1992 as 'the system by which companies are directed and controlled,' represents a topic that boosted interest within both the academic and professional communities. In the beginning, the term CG was predominantly used in the Anglo-American context, where it was principally referred to the functioning of the board of directors within the listed companies. In fact, the discussion pertaining CG began with the introduction of the American *public company* in the twentieth-century US public company, which led to the neat separation between control and ownership due to the pursuit of a specialised professional able to manage a pulverised capital of a company, whose ownership was spread among thousands of owners.[1]

The global privatisation wave began in the early 1990s and made CG an international matter. In this new economic context, the way of 'doing business' and the allocation of resources among companies, becoming the central entities for each national economy, were heavily influenced by the efficiency of the CG model adopted. The main peculiarity of companies was represented by their being a separated

DOI: 10.4324/9781003225805-4

entity from their owners (shareholders) who, in fact, let the control of their wealth to managers (Mintzberg, 1984).[2] Consequently, nations started to progressively issuing CG Codes of Best Practice, first of all, the *Cadbury Code* issued in the United Kingdom in 1992, which strongly emphasised the importance of minority shareholders, the independence of directors and the strengthening of the internal control system in order to more easily resolve conflicts of interest among stakeholders through a more efficient decision making process. The common aim to be reached at the national level was that of balancing different expectations gravitating around the company, in particular, the often discordant interests and needs of all stakeholders, such as employees, suppliers, shareholders and the public community.

In the new millennium, the economic context is characterised by the development of mass consumption and the absence of barriers among organisations that compete at a global level. More specifically, spatial and temporal barriers have been drastically removed to create higher competition fostered by a restless technological innovation process which has created new opportunities for global competitive and economic success. This new competition, no longer confined at national level, requires a substantial human and financial contribution. Regarding the former, top managers are required to be always more skilful than used to be a few decades ago, whereas regarding the latter, the stock and capital debt market have become the main sources of the financial resources required to run the business. In the supply chain, the business relationships have also changed as they are no longer exclusive to specific suppliers but refer to the entire supply chain as *competitive strategic alliances,* such as joint ventures, cooperative marketing, outsourcing and supply-chain partnership. All these vicissitudes require both external and internal changes. Regarding the former, companies need to establish new types of interactions with the external environment, whereas internally they have to reorganise their structure and processes in order to compete at global level and, simultaneously, satisfy stakeholders' needs in a fair, responsible and correct manner. In this regard, new networking strategies, based on collaboration rather than competition, have been implemented with the aim of increasing growth at global level. Competition, on the other hand, will no longer be among organisations but will be among networks. This has also fed a new view of global CG which is always oriented toward the obtainment of maximum results. However, recent financial scandals have hardly hit big corporations in different countries due to the *domino effect* (Bação et al. 2013), which was certainly facilitated by the lack of spatial and temporal barriers.

These negative results have emphasised the weakness of both the external and internal control systems, which should have been able to promptly detect any managers' misconducts and avoid the loss of savers' trust and faith in the economic system characterising each country. Therefore, there should be a national and international commitment to establish precise rules of good CG in order to pursue the aim of reducing the inability of national systems of CG to cope with the new global markets. In this regard, there have been substantial corporate reforms in each nation in order to homogenise the different models of CG driven by an international convergence hence creating the perfect CG model, transferable and adaptable to different national contexts. Unfortunately, the analysis of different CG models adopted at international level seems to reveal that there is still a long road to go to reach this desired convergence.

4.2 *One-Tier*, *Two-Tier* or the *Traditional* CG Model

The selection of the most suitable CG model is not an easy choice. However, if we had to choose at the end of the 1980s, our choice would have been an easy one due to the fact that the Japanese economic bubble did not burst yet, the English financial market was recovering from the collapse that occurred in the 1970s,[3] and the *takeover euphoria* in the United States was over. In this temporal context, the most appropriate CG model to adopt would have been the *two-tier* or dualistic. *What is the reason behind the choice to adopt the dualistic model?*

The *two-tier* board model, characterised by the presence of two separate bodies, the management board, and the supervisory board, allows to adopt a management strategy with a long-term time horizon. Furthermore, through a wise choice of allocating seats within the supervisory board, the dualistic system allows to maintain a network of business relationships with various subjects, including banks, which can support synergies within the business community. Therefore, the preference for the dualistic system is based on the crucial role played by the bank financing system rather than the Stock Exchange to obtain the financial resources necessary to carry out the activities within the company.

However, this preference for the two-tier model would not have lasted for long. In fact, only few years later, approximately in the mid-1990s, the dualistic model of CG would not have been the choice but rather the opposite one: the *one-tier* model of CG, which is characterised by the presence of one management body where executive directors carry out the management function of the company and non-executive directors exercise a supervisory function over the executive directors' activities.

In fact, in that period both Japan, with the economic bubble burst in 1991, and Germany, facing a difficult time after the fall of the Berlin wall and reunification process, were showing a clear sign of slowing down in comparison with the United States that was experiencing the 'economic miracle' characterised by a low unemployment and inflation rate.

Moreover, in the new millennium, the history of unanimity was experiencing the initial stages of a process that was certainly destined to be remembered as a 'new industrial revolution,' though the Internet and telecommunications, which provided for whoever had the intelligence to understand its epochal significance and the entrepreneurial spirit to take advantage of the great business opportunities offered as it was during the first industrial revolution.

Consequently, the best deals were done in the United States through the successful *venture capital* business formula in view of a timely listing on the stock exchange. Meanwhile, what was happening in Asia? By 1997, the currencies of the *four Asian tigers* (South Korea, Taiwan, Singapore and Hong Kong) had collapsed. The Monetary Fund was scrambling to have a healthy Anglo-Saxon style CG system accepted as a condition for its financial aid.

Unfortunately, in a few years, things changed again. The speculative bubble of Internet and telematics stocks burst in 2001, followed by a financial disaster as strong as that caused by the South Seas Bubble (Temin & Voth, 2004), although fortunately not with the same economic impact on investors, the *Enron* bankruptcy, accompanied by that of *WorldCom,* and in London by the financial crisis of *Equitable Life,* which demonstrated the unreliability of the *two-tier* CG structure.

At this point, we may think that the only option available in terms of CG structure would have been the traditional *Latin system* developed in different European countries, such as Italy, France, Belgium, Spain, Portugal and Greece, characterised by the presence of controlling shareholders, often represented by families, credit institutions or public bodies, with high strategic power guaranteed by voting agreements and share crossings. Therefore, banks and employees are simple external stakeholders with no management functions. However, the French scandal of *Vivendi* and that of the Italian *Parmalat* severely compromised the presumed awareness of stability of the traditional CG model. In conclusion, the perfect CG model does not exist.

However, the most suitable model is the system that provides companies with the widest choice and, therefore, allowing greater adaptability to the environment in which the company operates.

4.3 Features of a *Good* CG Model

Based on the validated assumption according to which a CG model able to adapt to each national context does not exist, however, we can identify some distinctive features of good CG, more specifically:

- a solid *corporate culture*: a process aimed at supervising how much of the CG culture is concretely understood and put into practice within the organisation must be established;
- *corporate ethics*: a valid CG model must be driven by accuracy and ethics due to the fact how activities are carried out under a social and environmental standpoint is also relevant in the pursuit of long-term goals;
- *skillful directors*: in order to manage organisations, especially large and complex ones, both executives and non-executives have to be extremely skillful in order to promptly identify companies' weaknesses and transform them into strengths;
- *transparency*: information must freely flow within the organisation and agreed on by anyone. In this regard, all stakeholders have to be able to obtain information in the same quantity and quality in order to be equally acknowledged regarding the company's vicissitudes;
- *fair treatment of shareholders and other stakeholders*: stakeholders ought not to be categorised in terms of importance as they should all equally contribute to the achievement of the long-term goals;
- a *balanced internal control system*: in order to reach its long-term goals, a company must establish an efficient internal control system and a clear division of powers among different subjects directly or indirectly involved in the organisation's activities;
- *practicality*: companies must concretely comply with laws and regulations and not just formally.

These elements should be considered as the main drivers of good CG regardless of the type of model analysed due to the fact that they may have prevented some of the main financial scandals occurred in the major big corporations around the world. On the other hand, the analysis of different CG models and different national contexts allowed the identification of some companies' vicissitudes, which proved that some models are more appropriate than others in those specific vicissitudes, among which:

- generational change: in family-controlled firms, the *two-tier* model allows a gradual generational transition by appointing new generation of directors and allowing the 'old' generation to maintain a role of direction and control by filling positions within the supervisory board. In fact, it is not uncommon for the president of the German board of directors (*Vorstand*), who reached a certain limit of age, to fill the role of chairman in the supervisory board (*Aufsichtsrat*). In the dualistic system, family members fill controlling positions within the supervisory board, while the new generation of skillful and knowledgeable directors, whether belonging to the company's founding family or not, operate in the board of directors;
- crisis and growth situations: in case of a company has to carry out a reorganisation plan in order to deal with a temporary crisis situation, the two-tier system is particularly appropriate due to the fact the family members directly or indirectly involved in the controlling activities performed within the supervisory board can exercise continuous and effective control over the management's recovery plan and activities. Another case may involve the organisational effort of reviewing restructuring processes due to a phase of rapid dimensional growth that led the company to become larger and the previous control systems are no longer adequate;
- mergers and acquisitions: the dualistic system allows the achievement of an adequate balance between the ownership and management of merged and acquired companies. For instance, in case of a company acquires a family company in which a significant component of the value produced stems from the know-how of some members of the founder's family. In this case, it appears plausible that some of family members will have a role within the management board, supported and controlled by the new controlling shareholder. Alternatively, if the acquiring company is able to provide adequate management skills, it can allocate these resources to the management board while shareholders of the acquired company, owing technical and experiential assets, may give useful contribution to the supervisory board;
- turnover in the top management: the *two-tier* system can be a solution, at least transitory, to achieve a non-traumatic change in the top management. More specifically, the outgoing CEO may be appointed a position in the supervisory board, hence the company

can still take advantage of the experience gained throughout the years;

- state-owned companies: the dualistic system allows politicians, appointed to the supervisory board, to reserve a guiding role and to exercise appropriate 'levers' to ensure compliance without directly interfering with the management;
- holding company: in case of a corporate group, especially of large dimensions in terms of number of subsidiary companies, the holding company can be more efficiently and consistently operate through a single collegial management body, while for the subsidiary companies, the choice of the CG system to adopt will depend on their characteristics and those of the activities carried out;
- fast-growth sectors and firms: while in case of an important restructuring programme implemented to recover from a previous crisis, the dualistic model, through the supervisory board, can verify the correct implementation of the programme which, however, can lead to some degree of rigidity in case of either sectors or firms characterised by rapid growth. In fact, in these sectors, the main condition for success is flexibility where the *one-tier* or monistic structure can be definitely more effective as all the members of the board of directors share the same responsibilities and objectives, as well as ensuring that the control mechanisms properly functions through the appropriate committees.

An important aspect that came to light from the analysis of different national CG structures is represented by the fact that if you compare different CG models in order to select the most suitable one, you need to bear the risk of encountering a misleading nominalistic perspective. More specifically, formally different structures of CG can lead to equivalent results. Therefore, in the selection of a CG system, first of all, attention must be paid to the description of the functions to be carried out and, more importantly, who actually exercise those functions otherwise the structural components of the CG model adopted are reduced to sterile nominal notions.

Overall, "scholars agree that the role played by corporate governance mechanisms is likely to be affected by the quality of the legal systems in which firms operate" (Mechelli and Cimini 2019: 203). However, the investigation of different CG models should be based on economic and social factors characterising each specific national context, therefore, the comparison should be made among country systems rather than CG models adopted in each country. In fact, there is not so much difference among the same type of CG models adopted in different countries. What makes the difference is the quantity and, above all, the quality of improvements made to these models by each country system in order to face the increasing international competition and, at the same time, boost company growth by increasing national and foreign investments. The empirical research conducted on the adoption of different CG models highlighted the need to evaluate the impact of institutions and regulations on each country system, bearing in mind there is no absolute best model of CG but there is a CG model that is more suitable for the historical, legislative, economic, financial, political, social and cultural evolution fostered in each country system. We may conclude by saying that the best CG model is the one that offers the widest freedom of choice to all stakeholders of the economic system.

Notes

1 Adam Smith (*The Wealth of Nations*, 1776) claimed that 'Being managers of other people's money rather than their own, it cannot be expected that they (managers) should watch over it with the same anxious vigilance, which (they would) watch over their own. Negligence and profusion, therefore, must always prevail, more or less, in the management of the affairs of such a company.'
2 Mintzteber states that by increasing the number of shareholders to increase companies' dimension, the consequent pulverised ownership of the companies inevitably leads to their weak control, which is concretely exercised by the management.
3 Between 1970 and 1979, the inflation rate had an average value of 12.4%, reaching its peak of 26.6% in 1975, while the average unemployment rate was of 4.1%.

References

Bação, P. , Maia Domingues, J. & Portugal Duarte, A. (2013). Financial crisis and domino effect. In J. S. Andrade, M. C. N. Simões , I. Stošić , D. Erić and H. Hanić (Eds.). *Managing Structural Changes-Trends and Requirements*. Belgrado: Institute of Economic Sciences (pp. 199–213). Portugal: Faculty of Economics of the University of Coimbra

Mechelli, A., & Cimini, R. (2019). Corporate governance, legal systems and value relevance of fair value estimates. Empirical evidence from the EU banking sector. *Spanish Journal of Finance and Accounting/Revista Española de Financiación y Contabilidad, 48*(2), 203–223.

Mintzberg, H. (1984). Who should control the corporation?. *California Management Review, 27*(1), 90–115.

Temin, P., & Voth, H. J. (2004). Riding the south sea bubble. *American Economic Review, 94*(5), 1654–1668.

Conclusion

Corporate governance (CG) 'involves a set of relationships between a company's management, its board, its shareholders and other stakeholders' (OECD 2015: 9) has been the object of an international substantial debate over the last two decades, especially due to a series of events occurred at a global level such as the corporate scandals of colossal dimensions, the globalisation of financial markets, the growing importance of institutional investors in terms of ownership of companies' shares, the increase in cross-border mergers and acquisitions, the listing of companies on foreign stock markets rather than in the country of origin. All these events have had a huge impact at the global level both at academic and professional level. Regarding the former, CG has become a very interdisciplinary topic where studies belonging to different academic areas such as business law, economics, sociology and history converge towards a fluid subject in terms of research and theoretical debate. Regarding the latter, professionals have to constantly train to increase their skills and knowledge to confront an increasingly internationalised topic.

Corporate governance models stem from the cultural, historical, ethical, political, religious and institutional development reached in each country where the interaction of various environmental factors also plays a crucial role in the enrichment of these models. More specifically, the strengths and weaknesses characterising each national environment where companies operate, in fact, shape the peculiarities of the CG model that can only efficiently function in the specific environment or country system. Consequently, as environmental factors change, the features of the models have to be improved accordingly in order to promptly respond to those changes.

In this current dynamic world, the idea of a universal CG model is able to adapt to any type of company and, above all, to any external environment in terms of economic, social, political, jurisdictional aspects, represents, unfortunately, a mere utopia. This was confirmed by the

DOI: 10.4324/9781003225805-102

comparative analysis conducted on the CG models utilised internationally, respectively, the *one-tier*, *two-tier* and *traditional* structure. The investigation revealed the strengths and weaknesses of each model led to the conclusion that the characteristics of each country system can allow either the development or the failure of the CG models available. On the other hand, the analysis revealed some principles on which each model ought to lay its foundations, more specifically developing a strong corporate culture and ethics; providing the company with skilful directors; treating both shareholders and other stakeholders fairly, implementing a balanced and efficient internal control system; concretely comply with laws and regulations; ensuring a high degree of transparency in the circulation of information which has to be equally provided to all the stakeholders involved in the company's activities.

Certainly, the best way to stimulate the adoption of good governance structures and behaviours is to that based on the improvement of the level of transparency in all the variables involved. In particular, transparency has to be guaranteed within the ownership structures of companies. However, the presence of shell companies, trust companies and business groups does not support the increase of transparency which is also to be referred to laws, regulations, and institutional bodies responsible for their drafting and application. In addition, transparency has to be the foundational principle for directors' and intermediaries' activities and remuneration and, last but not least, transparency must guide the financial market and the taxation system.

However, those in power can be strongly tempted to ensure that transparency does not increase due to the fact that ambiguity is considered one of the bases of power and of many opportunistic behaviours. Not transparent activities and behaviours lead to high transaction costs and, more importantly, the spread of a sense of inequity and viscosity of the entire economic system that frustrates the spirit of initiative and loyal and genuine cooperation among people, companies and public institutions.

Companies have to accept the fact that their responsibilities go beyond the creation of wealth for the shareholders and, at the same time, shareholders have to play a crucial role in ensuring it.

I do hope that the good CG principles and behaviours highlighted will not be reaming at the embryonal stage as the world in which we live has shown us so far.

Reference

OECD. (2015). G20/OECD Principles of Corporate Governance. OECD Publishing, Paris. http://dx.doi.org/10.1787/9789264236882-en

Index

Printed in the United States
by Baker & Taylor Publisher Services